TO ORDER MORE BOOKS, OR TO SEE OUR OTHER RESOURCES, PLEASE GO TO:

WWW.JACOBREEVE.ORG

LANGUAGE OF GOD SERIES
BOOK TWO

GOD SPEAKS through HEBREW CULTURE

ANCIENT HEBREW KNOWLEDGE EVERY CHRISTIAN NEEDS TO KNOW

Jacob Reeve

School of Jesus
Copyright 2011 Jacob Reeve

All rights reserved. Written permission must be secured from the author to use or reproduce any part of this book, except for brief and critical reviews or articles.

School of Jesus website: www.intheschoolofjesus.com
Jacob Reeve website: www.jacobreeve.com

Cover Design and Layout by Jacob Reeve

Unless otherwise indicated, all scripture quotations are taken from the New American Standard Bible,
Copyright 1960, 1962, 1963, 1968, 1971, 1972, 1973, 1975, 1977 by The Lockman Foundation.

Italics or bold type in scripture references are for emphasis only.

Printed in the United States of America.

CONTENTS

INTRODUCTION

SECTION 1
GOD SPEAKS THROUGH THE RABBINIC CULTURE

SECTION 2
GOD'S PARABLES IN HEBREW PATRIARCHS

SECTION 3
GOD SPEAKS THROUGH THE HEBREW CONCEPT OF COVENANT

SECTION 4
GOD SPEAKS THROUGH HEBREW LANGUAGE

SECTION 5
GOD SPEAKS THROUGH HEBREW WORDS

SECTION 6
GOD SPEAKS THROUGH HIS FEASTS

SECTION 7
GOD SPEAKS THROUGH HIS HOUSE

Introduction

According to UNESCO, the United Nations Educational, Scientific and Cultural Organization, approximately 26 percent of the world's adult population today is completely illiterate. Many estimate under 30% of the world population since the time of Christ has had access to the *written* scriptures and less than 40% of these have been literate. If these numbers are accurate, only around 12% of the world population over the last 2000 years has had any real access to the *written Scriptures*. This would be a major problem if God only communicated to people who had access to the Bible.

Imagine for a moment you were with God before the creation of the world. How did the Trinity communicate to One Another before mankind was created? Do you suppose they used the English language? Do you suppose they used human vocabulary at all? How do ageless, omniscient Beings communicate?

There are undoubtedly endless things God desires to communicate with us as individuals and with mankind as a whole. The disciples speaking in dozens of languages on the day of pentecost shows us that God is truly the master of our dialects. Yet while He does often use our native language to communicate to us as individuals, a brief survey of history ought to convince us that He certainly doesn't restrain His speech to the confines of our temporal understanding. We will see that His speech both penetrates and transcends the levels of understanding within each generation. His speech is like rivers of wine that flow just below the surface of our cultures, each having its own color and flavor. Each river continues to flow waiting for the generations to discover and tap the endless springs of life that flow from within.

Long before our earthly vocabularies were invented, God was already communicating with "words" that contain both the power to ignite time and space and outlive the eons of man's understanding. While God does often speak to us personally within the confines of our vocabularies, He also speaks Universally in ways that transcend the fleeting knowledge of the generations of man.

It might be surprising to some that English isn't God's primary language. Taking everything into consideration, I believe God speaks in ways so fundamental, so simple and so universal that we, in the busy legalities of our religious close-mindedness, often miss what He is saying.

Might it be, that we are placing a great handicap on the reception of His Voice by insisting that it be confined to our vocabulary? Might it be that God speaks and has been speaking a different language than we are familiar with? What if He doesn't really speak English that much at all? What if our English Bibles and English Church services were merely our attempts to relate to Him in our own understanding? I am not saying anything is wrong with this, in fact I expect He enjoys our attempts to define and explain Him. I am merely trying to bring up a point that God's communication goes back to time long before the English language was ever invented. The Word of God is a subject so much larger than the confines of any one human vocabulary.

The patriarchs, prophets and apostles knew God. They KNEW Him! They did not know Him vicariously through the writings of others, they knew Him themselves. They were often literate in a number of His universal languages. In the following chapters we will attempt to reveal the many means through which God has spoken and continues to speak both universally and individually.

Each one of the chapters of this book could easily be turned into an entire book. And many have indeed authored volumes on each of these topics. However, the goal of this series is not to create an endless examination of the subjects. Instead, each chapter was created to be a doorway that opens its readers to yet another pillar of understanding. The goal is to open all the doors of God's voice to you so that you are fully introduced to the knowledge and vastness of His speech.

There is an art of prophecy but there is also the science of prophecy. The art deals with the ability to hear God personally and presently for a specific situation. The science deals with knowing God truly, understanding how He HAS spoken, and understanding His Wisdom and His Word through the ages. The apostle John writes, "In the beginning was the Word... and the Word became flesh and dwelt among us..." He understood the true Science or Nature of God's Word. The wise men saw signs in the stars and they knew the Christ was about to be born in Bethlehem. There was a science they had found to knowing the one true God. This book series will introduce its readers to both the Science and the Art of knowing God and His voice.

May God grant you intimacy and true knowing through the revelations found within.

1

HE SPEAKS THROUGH RABBINIC CULTURE

THE NEW TESTAMENT IS A JEWISH WORK

In the last book we found that Christ trumps all former and lesser revelation about God. Christ is the subject of the Scriptures. Now that this has been established we can go back and really understand what the Scriptures say about Christ.

Because the reader undoubtedly uses the New Testament as a source of theology, it is important to know the context the New Testament was written in. As Gentile Christians we often don't realize that the entire New Testament is a Hebrew work. Just about everything that is described in the New Testament has Hebrew roots. Without understanding these Hebrew roots, we are left to our own imaginations for the interpretation and application of the teachings and customs delivered to us in the New Testament. One of the names of God is "the God of Israel." That is a big deal.

A study of the New Testament is a study of Jewish culture. Without knowing the Jewish culture and context of the New Testament, we will often mis-apply the revelation of the New Testament. This chapter seeks to unearth a number of the larger contextual misconceptions of the New Testament.

GOD USES THE NATION OF ISRAEL TO SPEAK TO US

God speaks to every generation in many ways but His primary language does not use human vocabulary. He has littered the human race with His word; Love portraits, letters and pictures delivered not through human words, but through interactions, human experience and history. One of the major ways He speaks to us is through the Nation of Israel.

Putting aside any judgments on the politics or ethics of modern day Israel, it is clear from Scripture that God has used Israel to speak in the past, and intends to continue to use the Nation to speak in the present and future.

And I will make you a great nation, And I will bless you, And make your name great; And so you shall be a blessing; ³And I will bless those who bless you, And the one who curses you I will curse. And in you all the families of the earth will be blessed." - Genesis 12:2-3

The passage above reveals God's initial purpose in creating the nation of Israel. According to this passage, what does God say He wants the Nation of Israel to be in relation to all the other nations of the earth?

"'...and you shall be to Me a kingdom of priests and a holy nation.' These are the words that you shall speak to the sons of Israel." - Exodus 19:6

A priest is someone who's primary job is to intercede and make atonement for others before God. If God originally wanted the entire nation of Israel to be priests, who do you think they were called to intercede for?

"*Also the foreigners who join themselves to the Lord, To minister to Him, and to love the name of the Lord, To be His servants, every one who keeps from profaning the sabbath And holds fast My covenant; ⁷ Even those I will bring to My holy mountain And make them joyful in My house of prayer. Their burnt* offerings and their sacrifices will be acceptable on My altar; For My house will be called a house of prayer for all the peoples." - Isaiah 56:6-7

In the passage above we find the Old Testament context for the phrase, "a house of prayer for all nations." This phrase was later quoted by Jesus as He was rebuking the pharisees for turning the priesthood into a money making business. Many people think that a "house of prayer for all nations" means the place we go to pray for all the nations, but what does this passage reveal is God's version of a house of prayer for all nations?

In the space provided under the following passages, please describe the purpose and/or effect Israel has on the nations.

"...Israel; I will also make you a light of the nations." - Isaiah 49:6

^{6} Keep [My commands] and do them, for that will be your wisdom and your understanding in the sight of the peoples [nations], who, when they hear all these statutes, will say, 'Surely this great nation is a wise and understanding people.' ^{7} For what great nation is there that has a god so near to it as the Lord our God is to us, whenever we call upon him? ^{8} And what great nation is there, that has statutes and rules so righteous as all this law that I set before you today? - Deuteronomy 4:2-8

CONTEXT BEGETS "KNOWING"

Almost everyone approaches God and the Scriptures through a veil or lens. We cannot help it. Some people see God through the lens of their denominational teachings, others through the lens of their own earthly fathers, others through the lens of the natural world and others through an obscure passage or two of scripture. As you should know by now, the New Testament affirms Christ as the veil or lens that removes all others. He is the only accurate view of God. We can label the lens that people view God through by the title, "the theological lens."

If you come to the Scriptures with a theological lens that paints the picture of an angry God, then you will generally only hear an angry and condemning voice coming from God. If your theological lens tells you that God only works through natural means, then you automatically disqualify any supernatural words He might speak to you. The point being, your theological lens effects the way you view God and hear God.

Lets look at the story of the Samaritan woman and Jesus for an example:

[19]*The woman *said to Him, "Sir, I perceive that You are a prophet. [20]Our fathers worshiped in this mountain, and you people say that in Jerusalem is the place where men ought to worship." [21]Jesus said to her, "Woman, believe Me, an hour is coming when neither in this mountain nor in Jerusalem will you worship the Father. [22]You worship what you do not know; we worship what we know, for salvation is from the Jews. [23]But an hour is coming, and now is, when the true worshipers will worship the Father in*

*spirit and truth; for such people the Father seeks to
be His worshipers. ²⁴God is Spirit, and those who
worship Him must worship in spirit and truth." ²⁵The
woman said to Him, "I know that Messiah is coming
(He who is called Christ); when that One comes, He
will declare all things to us." ²⁶ Jesus *said to her, "I
who speak to you am He." - John 4:19-26*

*After reading the passage above, please explain
how Jesus links "knowing" God with being Jewish
(vs. 22).*

What do you think He is saying by this?

      In the passage above, Jesus tells the woman,
"You worship what you do not know; we worship
what we know, for salvation is from the Jews." He is
essentially saying that one's worship is hindered if
they don't know the One True God and the
revelation of the One True God will come through
the Jewish Nation.

JESUS WAS A RABBI

      Jesus was a rabbi. If He is our Lord, it would
seem important to understand what it means for
Him to be a rabbi. From the days of Moses to the
days of the apostles, the entire Bible was either
written by Hebrews or by those who lived in Hebrew
culture. During the time of Jesus, "Rabbis" had
become the central figure of Hebrew life and
religion. The Rabbinic influence stretched into every
area of culture, bringing rabbinic thought, lifestyle,
education and tradition, with a variety of Rabbinic
terms and sayings. The New Testament is written in

context to the Rabbinic culture, using many Rabbinic terms and sayings in its pages.

Without understanding some of the intricacies of the Jewish Rabbinic culture, it is nearly impossible to understand the context of a lot of the New Testament and ultimately the context of Christ. Much of the meaning of the New Testament will be missed unless you understand the language and context behind it. In this chapter we will unveil a number of contextual revelations that might help you better understand New Testament Scripture and therefore God.

In the passages below, please highlight the one to whom the label "Rabbi" is given.

Peter *said to Jesus, "Rabbi, it is good for us to be here; let us make three tabernacles, one for You, and one for Moses, and one for Elijah." - Mark 9:5

And Jesus turned and saw them following, and *said to them, "What do you seek?" They said to Him, "Rabbi (which translated means Teacher), where are You staying?" - John 1:38

"...this man came to Jesus by night and said to Him, "Rabbi, we know that You have come from God as a teacher; for no one can do these signs that You do unless God is with him." - John 3:2

THE RABBINIC STAGES OF LIFE

Mishnah Avot 5:21 tells us of "the stages of life" of a male Jew.

"At five years old [one is fit] for the [study of]

Scripture (written Torah), at ten years for [the study of] the Mishnah (Oral Torah), at thirteen for [the fulfilling of] the commandments, at fifteen for the Talmud, at eighteen for the bride-chamber, at twenty for pursuing [a calling], at thirty for authority, at forty for discernment, at fifty for counsel, at sixty to be an elder, at seventy for gray hairs, at eighty for special strength, at ninety for bowed back, and at a hundred a man is as one that has [already] died and passed away and ceased from the world." - Mishnah Avot 5:21

This text is from the Mishnah traditions taken from around the time of Jesus. - Trans. Danby, The Mishnah, p. 458.

After reading the previous passage, please list the 14 stages of Hebrew life below:

There are a number of important points that this passage unveils about the culture that Jesus was raised in:

The Rabbis taught that schooling was to begin at the early age of 5. This means Jesus went to school just like all the other little Hebrew boys and girls.

At age 10, they began studying the "Oral Torah" or the "traditions." (More on this in the next section.)

*Age 13 (The Bar Mitsvah or Bat Mitsvah) was the "age of accountability," meaning your parents were no longer responsible if you broke the commandments. "Mitzvah" means "Commandment." "Bat" and "Bar" are "Daughter" and "Son" respectively. When you turn 13 is when you are said to become a son or daughter of the commandment.

*Around age 18 is when marriage was expected

*Age 30 is when a man gained authority. In fact, it was said that you shouldn't eat the fruit of a tree until it is three years old, and likewise you should not eat the fruit (teaching) of a man until he is 30. This is why Jesus started His earthly teaching ministry at 30 (Nor did Joseph - Gen 41:46, the Levite priests - Num. 4:3, Saul - 1 Sam 13:1, David - 2 Sam 5:4, Ezekiel - Ez 1:1, & John the Baptist)

*Notice marriage was generally to take place before the pursuit of a career or the assumption of authority. This was unless an individual has a particular calling not to get married (like Jesus).

* Notice that 40 is when one can be respected for his discernment, at 50 one is respected for council, and 60 one is considered an elder. These are all Biblical terms.

[39] When they (Mary and Joseph) had performed everything according to the Law of the Lord, they returned to Galilee, to their own city of Nazareth. [40] The Child (Jesus) continued to grow and become

strong, increasing in wisdom; and the grace of God was upon Him. - Luke 2:39-40

During the early childhood of Jesus, the teachings of a Rabbi named Hillel influenced much of the region of Galilee where Jesus was raised. Many have said Hillel's teachings are very similar to Jesus'. The fact that Jesus was raised in Nazareth tells us that He likely studied under the influence of Rabbi Hillel.

If you are a natural or spiritual parent, one of the things you can do for your children is offer them a blessing at each one of these stages of life. At conception, during the time in the womb, at birth, childhood (age 5), pre-teen (age 10), adolescence (13), adulthood (18), pursuing career (20), authority (30), discernment (40), council (50), and Older age (60) (children bless parents at this stage). Receiving these blessings at these stages of life can help to provide you guidance and confirmation, affirming value and purpose in life.

THE TORAH

As you can gather from the previous section, the entire culture of the Jewish Orthodox people is built on the preservation of the Law. Starting at five years old. Jewish orthodox children spend their entire childhood learning and memorizing the Torah as the primary part of their education. At 12 or 13, they have their "bar mitzvah" or "Bat Mitzvah" which is a "coming of age" ceremony where they become responsible for their actions and become a "Child of the Commandment." At this point they, instead of their parents are said to be liable for their actions.

After Bar Mitzvah, the local Rabbi would often ask the most promising students to remain on under his tutelage as a disciple (student) as they study to become a rabbi themselves. Here, they would begin to move past the memorization of the Torah and into interpretation of how the Torah should be applied in their community. These were called students or "disciples."

TWO SETS OF TORAH: WRITTEN AND ORAL TRADITION

In Jewish culture there are two sets of Law or Torah. There is the Written Torah and the Oral Torah. The written torah is what we know as the first five books of the Old Testament, otherwise known as "the Pentateuch," or "the Law," or "Moses." The "Oral Torah" is basically the traditional interpretations and applications of "the Law" to be practiced and applied by the people of God.

Both the Written Torah and the Oral Torah were meticulously preserved for many centuries through the religious education system of memorization by the entire culture of the Jewish people. Most orthodox Jewish children continue this tradition of preserving the law of Moses through the practice of memorization to this day.

THE WRITTEN TORAH

Most historians agree that the Pentateuch was first compiled into one book, as it was translated and written into Koine Greek and put into one volume in the 3rd Century BC. This Greek Old Testament work is called "the Septuagint."

Traditional History tells us that King Ptolemy II sponsored the translation for use by the many Alexandrian Jews who were fluent in Koine Greek, but not in Hebrew. According to the record in the Talmud:

"King Ptolemy once gathered 72 Elders. He placed them in 72 chambers, each of them in a separate one, without revealing to them why they were summoned. He entered each one's room and said, 'Write for me the Torah of Moshe your teacher.' God put it in the heart of each one to translate identically as all the others did."

This is really amazing. This is where our current copies of the Old Testament came from. A Gentile King who appointed 72 Jewish elders to write down what they had memorized as children and reportedly, they all wrote the exact same thing word for word. Thats a sign and wonder to many as well as a testimony to the Jewish methods of study and memorization!

THE ORAL TORAH: YOKES, BURDENS & BINDING & LOOSING

Each rabbi would have their own interpretation and adherence to the written law of Moses. In the sermon on the mount we find Rabbi Jesus' interpretation and application of Moses' law. When these interpretations were agreed upon by the elders of a town or region, they would begin to be taught as oral tradition, or oral torah. The oral traditions were viewed as the law itself, meaning if you broke the tradition, it was equally as if you were also breaking the law the tradition was founded upon.

The elders in a town had the authority to come together to adjust the level to which their people were called to observe their traditions and laws. This was called binding and loosing. They would either bind the people to observing some law, or loose them from observing some law.

In the space provided under the passages below, please note the revelation the passage offers in light of what you learned in the paragraphs above.

I will give you the keys of the kingdom of heaven; and whatever you bind on earth shall have been bound in heaven, and whatever you loose on earth shall have been loosed in heaven." - Matthew 16:19

Truly I say to you, whatever you bind on earth shall have been bound in heaven; and whatever you loose on earth shall have been loosed in heaven. [19] Again I say to you, that if two of you agree on earth about anything that they may ask, it shall be done for them by My Father who is in heaven. [20] For where two or three have gathered together in My name, I am there in their midst." - Matthew 18:18-20

During the time of the incarnation of Christ, one of the major grey areas of the law was the observance of the Sabbath. To what level did God want us not to work on the Sabbath? - The Old Testament doesn't exactly say. It was up to the elders of each town to decide how they would observe the Sabbath. The pharisees and elders in Jerusalem had taught it was unlawful to heal on the Sabbath, but in Galilee where Jesus had come from, Hillel and the pharisees there had taught that it was lawful to heal at any time.

" On another Sabbath [Jesus] entered the synagogue and was teaching; and there was a man there whose right hand was withered. ⁷ The scribes and the Pharisees were watching [Jesus] closely to see if He healed on the Sabbath, so that they might find reason to accuse Him. ⁸ But He knew what they were thinking, and He said to the man with the withered hand, "Get up and come forward!" And he got up and came forward. ⁹ And Jesus said to them, "I ask you, is it lawful to do good or to do harm on the Sabbath, to save a life or to destroy it?" ¹⁰ After looking around at them all, He said to him, "Stretch out your hand!" And he did so; and his hand was restored. ¹¹ But they themselves were filled with rage, and discussed together what they might do to Jesus." - Luke 6:6-11

According to the passage above, why were the Pharisees enraged at Jesus?

Every rabbi had a following of disciples. Each rabbi would teach his disciples to observe his own interpretation of the law. When a disciple followed a rabbi in this manner, the disciple was said to have taken on the rabbi's yoke or burden.

"Take My yoke upon you and learn from Me, for I am gentle and humble in heart, and you will find rest for your souls. ³⁰ For My yoke is easy and My burden is light." - Matthew 11:29-30

What does Jesus reveal about His own style of discipleship in the passage above?

²⁸ *"For it seemed good to the Holy Spirit and to us to lay upon you no greater burden than these essentials: ²⁹ that you abstain from things sacrificed to idols and from blood and from things strangled and from fornication; if you keep yourselves free from such things, you will do well. Farewell." Acts 15:28-29*

According to the passage above, what three burdens does James lay on the newly formed Church in Jerusalem?

"The Pharisees and some of the scribes gathered around Him when they had come from Jerusalem, ² and had seen that some of His disciples were eating their bread with impure hands, that is, unwashed. ³ (For the Pharisees and all the Jews do not eat unless they carefully wash their hands, thus observing the traditions of the elders; ⁴ and when they come from the market place, they do not eat unless they cleanse themselves; and there are many other things which they have received in order to observe, such as the washing of cups and pitchers and copper pots.) ⁵ The Pharisees and the scribes *asked Him, "Why do Your disciples not walk according to the tradition of the elders, but eat their bread with impure hands?" ⁶ And He said to them, "Rightly did Isaiah prophesy of you hypocrites, as it is written: 'This people honors Me with their lips, But their heart is far away from Me. ⁷ 'But in vain do they worship Me, Teaching as doctrines the precepts of men.'⁸ Neglecting the commandment of God, you hold to the tradition of men." ⁹ He was also saying to them, "You are experts at setting aside the

commandment of God in order to keep your tradition. [10] For Moses said, 'Honor your father and your mother'; and, 'He who speaks evil of father or mother, is to be put to death'; [11] but you say, 'If a man says to his father or his mother, whatever I have that would help you is Corban (that is to say, given to God),' [12] you no longer permit him to do anything for his father or his mother; [13] thus invalidating the word of God by your tradition which you have handed down; and you do many things such as that." - Mark 7:1-13

In the passage above, what is the contrast that Jesus makes between the Pharisee's oral traditions and the law of Moses?

THE MINIMUM REQUIREMENTS OF A CONVERT TO JUDAISM

Decades before Christ's incarnation, the question arose as to what a Gentile convert to Judaism needed to observe as a minimum requirement of the Law. This question was discussed and the elders and leaders agreed on three universal minimum observances focusing on Murder, Fornication & Idolatry. This is exactly what happened in Acts 15 when the question was brought to the church about what minimum requirements of the Law the new Gentile converts should continue to observe.

"[13]After they had stopped speaking, James answered, saying,"...Then it seemed good to the apostles and the elders, with the whole church, to choose men from among them to send to Antioch with Paul and Barnabas—Judas called Barsabbas, and Silas, leading men among the brethren, [23] and they sent this letter by them, "The apostles and the brethren who are elders, to the brethren in Antioch and Syria and Cilicia who are from the Gentiles, greetings. [24] "Since we have heard that some of our number to whom we gave no instruction have disturbed you with their words, unsettling your souls, [25] it seemed good to us, having become of one mind, to select men to send to you with our beloved Barnabas and Paul, [26] men who have risked their lives for the name of our Lord Jesus Christ. [27] "Therefore we have sent Judas and Silas, who themselves will also report the same things by word of mouth. [28] "For it seemed good to the Holy Spirit and to us to lay upon you no greater burden than these essentials: [29] that you abstain from things sacrificed to idols and from blood and from things strangled and from fornication; if you keep yourselves free from such things, you will do well. Farewell. [30] So when they were sent away, they went down to Antioch; and having gathered the congregation together, they delivered the letter." - Acts 15:13, 22-30

In the passage above, please highlight the words, "the apostles and the elders," along with the four things James requires the Gentile converts in the church of Antioch to observe.

RABBINICAL LIFESTYLE

Rabbi's were all expected to have trades like blacksmithing, carpentry or tent making that they would do wherever they went. When a rabbi would come to a new town, he would check in with those who operated in his same trade and work with them. Rabbis were held in the highest honor among all the people so communities readily accommodated their presence and townspeople sometimes even fought over who got to host them, which included food and lodging. When a rabbi found a host, he would stay with them the entire duration of his visit. Because rabbis walked and traveled so much, their disciples were said to be "in the dust of their rabbi." This meant being subject to his teachings and travels.

In the passages below, please highlight any words or phrases that parallel the information given in the previous paragraph.

"Is not this the carpenter, the son of Mary, and brother of James and Joses and Judas and Simon? Are not his sisters here with us?" And they took offense at Him." - Mark 6:3

"...and because [Paul] was of the same trade, he stayed with them and they were working, for by trade they were tent-makers." - Acts 18:3

"Now after this the Lord appointed seventy others, and sent them in pairs ahead of Him to every city and place where He Himself was going to come. ^{2} And He was saying to them, "The harvest is plentiful, but the laborers are few; therefore beseech the Lord of the harvest to send out laborers into His harvest. ^{3} Go; behold, I send you out as lambs in the midst of wolves. ^{4} Carry no money belt, no bag, no shoes; and greet no one on the way. ^{5} Whatever house you enter, first say, 'Peace be to this house.' ^{6} If a man of peace is there, your peace will rest on him; but if not, it will return to you. ^{7} Stay in that house, eating and drinking what they give you; for the laborer is worthy of his wages. Do not keep *moving from house to house. ⁸ Whatever city you enter and they receive you, eat what is set before you; ⁹ and heal those in it who are sick, and say to them, 'The kingdom of God has come near to you.' ¹⁰ But whatever city you enter and they do not receive you, go out into its streets and say, ¹¹ 'Even the dust of your city which clings to our feet we wipe off in protest against you; yet be sure of this, that the kingdom of God has come near.' - Luke 10:1-11*

And as for those who do not receive you, as you go out from that city, shake the dust off your feet as a testimony against them." Luke 9:5

But they shook off the dust of their feet in protest against them and went to Iconium. Acts 13:51

A RABBI'S PARABLES AND WISDOM

Jesus wasn't the only one who spoke in parables. It was common for many wise men, rabbis and prophets to develop their own parables to illustrate and deliver their teachings.

"I have also spoken to the prophets, And I gave numerous visions, And through the prophets I gave parables." - Hosea 12:10

According to the passage above, what two ways does God like to speak through prophets?

Jesus was obviously a very gifted teacher and His favorite subject matter was undoubtedly the "kingdom of God." Almost all of His parables began with, "the kingdom of God is like..." One key to unlocking the meanings of His parables is understanding that in a kingdom, the King and his kingdom are one. When Jesus says, "the kingdom of God is like a man," or "like a dragnet" or "like a merchant." God is the object of the teaching. He is the Man, the Dragnet, the Merchant... The kingdom centers on its King. These are all teachings about God.

In the following passages (all from Matthew 13) please highlight and label what God is likened to and what the passage teaches about Him.

33 He spoke another parable to them, "The kingdom of heaven is like leaven, which a woman took and hid in three pecks of flour until it was all leavened." - Matthew 13:33

44 "The kingdom of heaven is like a treasure hidden in the field, which a man found and hid again; and from joy over it he goes and sells all that he has and buys that field. 45 "Again, the kingdom of heaven is like a merchant seeking fine pearls, 46 and upon finding one pearl of great value, he went and sold all that he had and bought it. - Matthew 13:44-45

47 "Again, the kingdom of heaven is like a dragnet cast into the sea, and gathering fish of every kind; 48 and when it was filled, they drew it up on the beach; and they sat down and gathered the good fish into containers, but the bad they threw away. - Matthew 13:47-48

PARABLES OF TRUE RICHES

In the Hebrew culture during the incarnation of Christ, the pharisees taught that true wealth was said to be measured by ones knowledge of the Torah (God's law). The kingdom of God was where God's law ruled and for this reason, one's knowledge of the law was thought to indicate one's true heavenly possession of the true riches of the Kingdom of God.

"One person pretends to be rich, yet has nothing; another pretends to be poor, yet has great wealth."
- Proverbs 13:7

[9] I tell you, use worldly wealth to gain friends for yourselves, so that when it is gone, you will be welcomed into eternal dwellings. [11] ...So if you have not been trustworthy in handling worldly wealth, who will trust you with true riches? - Luke 16:9-11

[11] So I ask, did they (the Jews) stumble in order that they might fall? By no means! Rather through their trespass salvation has come to the Gentiles, so as to make Israel jealous. [12] Now if their trespass means riches for the world, and if their failure means riches for the Gentiles, how much more will their full inclusion mean! - Romans 11:11-12

"...Poor, yet making many rich; having nothing, and yet possessing everything." - 2 Corinthians 6:10

Jesus also sometimes used parable-style questions or stories to rebuke pharisees indirectly. In Luke 16 we find Jesus teaching two major parables using rich men as His subject. As we survey these teachings once again, this time remembering that in rabbinic culture, true riches were equated to the knowledge of the Torah, we see a whole new meaning emerge.

¹⁹"Now there was a rich man, and he habitually dressed in purple and fine linen, joyously living in splendor every day. ²⁰And a poor man named Lazarus (means "God will help) was laid at his gate, covered with sores, ²¹and longing to be fed with the crumbs which were falling from the rich man's table; besides, even the dogs were coming and licking his sores. ²²Now the poor man died and was carried away by the angels to Abraham's bosom; and the rich man also died and was buried. ²³In Hades he lifted up his eyes, being in torment, and *saw Abraham far away and Lazarus in his bosom. ²⁴And he cried out and said, 'Father Abraham, have mercy on me, and send Lazarus so that he may dip the tip of his finger in water and cool off my tongue, for I am in agony in this flame.' ²⁵But Abraham said, 'Child, remember that during your life you received your good things, and likewise Lazarus bad things; but now he is being comforted here, and you are in agony. ²⁶And besides all this, between us and you there is a great chasm fixed, so that those who wish to come over from here to you will not be able, and that none may cross over from there to us.' ²⁷And he said, 'Then I beg you, father, that you send him to my father's house— ²⁸for I have five brothers—in order that he may warn them, so that they will not also come to this place of torment.' ²⁹But Abraham *said, 'They have Moses and the Prophets; let them hear them.' ³⁰But he said, 'No, father Abraham, but if someone goes to them from the dead, they will repent!' ³¹But he said to him, 'If they do not listen to Moses and the Prophets, they will not be persuaded even if someone rises from the dead.'"

According to the passage above, what was Jesus saying to the pharisees who were "rich" in the Torah? Who do you suppose are the ones who Lazarus represents?

RABBINIC PRAYERS & BLESSINGS

Understanding Rabbinic prayers and blessings unlocks New Testament context. Judaism's central prayer is called the "Amidah" which is literally means "the Standing" prayer as every observant Jew stands to face Jerusalem three times a day (morning, noon and evening) to recite this prayer. It is also sometimes called "Shmoneh Esreh" which means "the Eighteen" in reference to the original number of constituent blessings. Since before the incarnation of Christ, the Amidah has been the central prayer of the Jewish liturgy. The prayer, among others, is found in the siddur, the traditional Jewish prayer book. (NOTE: See # 2 at end of book notes for full version Amidah)

Variations of the Amidah have been applied and recited at various services, events and festivals. It was said that each Rabbi had his own shortened version of the Amidah in case he was traveling or otherwise unable to pray the entire prayer, which generally takes about 10 minutes. Each rabbi would teach his personally shortened version to his disciples. This is what the New Testament records Jesus doing at two separate times, once at the sermon on the mount and then later when the disciples asked Him how to pray.

9"Pray, then, in this way:'Our Father who is in heaven, Hallowed be Your name. 10'Your kingdom come. Your will be done, On earth as it is in heaven. 11'Give us this day our daily bread. 12'And forgive us our debts, as we also have forgiven our debtors. 13'And do not lead us into temptation, but deliver us from evil. [For Yours is the kingdom and the power and the glory forever. Amen.']" - Matthew 6:9-13

"It happened that while Jesus was praying in a certain place, after He had finished, one of His disciples said to Him, "Lord, teach us to pray just as John also taught his disciples." ²And He said to them, "When you pray, say: 'Father, hallowed be Your name. Your kingdom come. ³'Give us each day our daily bread. ⁴'And forgive us our sins, For we ourselves also forgive everyone who is indebted to us. And lead us not into temptation.'" - Luke 11:1-4

BLESSING & THANKSGIVING

The word "bless" is "barak" in Hebrew. In Genesis 24:11 we read, "And he made the camels "kneel down" outside the city." The phrase "kneel down" is the Hebrew verb ברך (B.R.K), the very same word translated as "bless." The concrete meaning of ברך is to kneel down. It paints a similar picture of the idea of praise and worship. The extended meaning of this word is to pronounce and place credit, honor or value on another. God "blesses" us by providing for our needs and we in turn "bless" God by giving him credit and thanksgiving.

In the New Testament Greek, the word for bless is "eulogeo" which can be interpreted, "praise, celebrate, bless, make happy, or bestow favor."

Many Christians say grace before a meal as a tradition but mistakenly bless the food instead of the One who provided it. This might be due to translations of the Bible that do not take into account the Jewish customs that Jesus practiced.

"And as they were eating, Jesus took bread, and blessed [it], and brake [it], and gave [it] to the

disciples, and said, Take, eat; this is my body." - Matthew 26:26 (KJV)

Notice the King James version inserts [it] when the text does not contain [it]. The blessing that Jesus gave was to God, not to the bread. Below you will find a more accurate picture:

While they were eating, Jesus took some bread, and after a blessing, He broke it and gave it to the disciples, and said, "Take, eat; this is My body." - Matthew 26:26 (NASB)

It was never tradition to bless food or to give thanks to the food. Blessing God and giving Him thanks before we eat shows gratitude and recognition for His benevolence and grace.

[4] "For everything created by God is good, and nothing is to be rejected if it is received with gratitude; [5] for it is sanctified by means of the word of God and prayer." - 1 Timothy 4:4-6

What does the passage above give as the reason for giving thanks and blessing God for food?

An example of a Jewish blessing before or after a meal.

"Blessed are You, L-rd our G-d, King of the universe, who, in His goodness, provides sustenance for the entire world with grace, with kindness, and with mercy. He gives food to all flesh, for His kindness is everlasting. Through His great goodness to us continuously we do not lack [food], and may we never lack food, for the sake of His great Name. For He, benevolent G-d, provides nourishment and

sustenance for all, does good to all, and prepares food for all His creatures whom He has created, as it is said: You open Your hand and satisfy the desire of every living thing. Blessed are You, L-rd, who provides food for all."

Notice how a blessing is directed at someone, giving them thanks, credit and praise for their part in your happiness.

BLESSINGS AND CURSES

God honors the prayers, declarations and pronouncements of His children, especially those who have proven good stewards of His grace. There are countless examples of God inspiring and/or honoring the blessing of individuals, leaders, children, kings and priests as they are offered by those in authority. There are also many examples of God honoring the curses made by His servants.

In the space provided below each of the following passages, please make note of the things you learn about blessing and cursing.

"I will bless those who bless you, and whoever curses you I will curse; and all peoples on earth will be blessed through you." - Genesis 12:3

"To Adam he said, "Because you listened to your wife and ate fruit from the tree about which I commanded you, 'You must not eat from it,' "Cursed is the ground because of you; through painful toil you will eat food from it all the days of your life." - Genesis 3:17

"The Lord smelled the pleasing aroma and said in his heart: "Never again will I curse the ground because of humans, even though every inclination of the human heart is evil from childhood. And never again will I destroy all living creatures, as I have done." - Genesis 8:21

"Do not blaspheme God or curse the ruler of your people." - Exodus 22:28

"[Balak, king of Moab said to Balaam,] '...Now, therefore, please come, curse this people for me since they are too mighty for me; perhaps I may be able to defeat them and drive them out of the land. For I know that he whom you bless is blessed, and he whom you curse is cursed.' But God said to Balaam, 'Do not go with them. You must not put a curse on those people, because they are blessed.'" - Numbers 22:12

NOTE: In Numbers 5:11-31 God tells the Israelite priests how to pronounce curses over people who would bear false witness in court. It is too long of a section to include here but well worth studying.

"[12] On the next day, when they had left Bethany, [Jesus] became hungry. [13] Seeing at a distance a fig tree in leaf, He went to see if perhaps He would find anything on it; and when He came to it, He found nothing but leaves, for it was not the season for figs. [14] He said to it, "May no one ever eat fruit from you again!" And His disciples were listening... [19] When evening came, they would go out of the city. [20] As they were passing by in the morning, they saw the

fig tree withered from the roots up. ^{21} Being reminded, Peter *said to Him, "Rabbi, look, the fig tree which You cursed has withered." ^{22} And Jesus answered saying to them, "Have faith in God. ^{23} Truly I scy to you, whoever says to this mountain, 'Be taken up and cast into the sea,' and does not doubt in his heart, but believes that what he says is going to happen, it will be granted him. ^{24} Therefore I say to you, all things for which you pray and ask, believe that you have received them, and they will be granted you. ^{25} Whenever you stand praying, (standing prayer) forgive, if you have anything against anyone, so that your Father who is in heaven will also forgive you your transgressions." - Mark 11:12-25

"[Jesus said] ^{13} If the house is worthy, give it your blessing of peace. But if it is not worthy, take back your blessing of peace. ^{14} Whoever does not receive you, nor heed your words, as you go out of that house or that city, shake the dust off your feet. ^{15} Truly I scy to you, it will be more tolerable for the land of Sodom and Gomorrah in the day of judgment than for that city." - Matthew 10:13-15

In the passage above, many would assume Jesus is leading His disciples to curse their enemies. I do not believe this is completely true for he earlier says, "Bless those who curse you, pray for those who mistreat you" -Luke 6:28. I do not believe they are being encouraged to harbor a spirit of malice or revenge in their hearts but more of a warning of the value and authority of the message they carry.

Note that blessings and curses literally are spoken declarations and statements pronounced over a person, place or thing. As priests and sons, we have tremendous authority to bless and to curse and the pronouncements we make will often be honored by God. The more authority or agreement these blessings or curses find with God and/or man, the more power and effect they have on a person place or thing. Many people, even believers walk around weighed down by many curses even to this day, believing things about themselves that God has never spoken over them. Be careful what you pronounce over yourself and others. Also be careful what you agree with over yourself and others.

SICKNESS AND THE CURSE OF THE LAW

It might be surprising to some that God often used the Jewish patriarchs and prophets to heal the sick and diseased before the incarnation of Christ. God healed through Abraham (Gen.20:1-18), through Moses (Num.21:4-9), through the Eli (1 Sam 1:9-20), Elijah (1 Kings 17:17-24), Elisha (2 Kings 5:1-14), Daniel (Dan. 4:34, 36), and many others.

During the incarnation of Christ, often when people were sick or diseased, they were said to be under "the curse of the law." This is in reference back to Deuteronomy

"If you fully obey the Lord your God and carefully follow all his commands I give you today, the Lord your God will set you high above all the nations on earth. 2 All these blessings will come on you and accompany you if you obey the Lord your God..." - Deuteronomy 28:1-2 *(it goes on to list many types of blessing)*

"However, if you do not obey the Lord your God and do not carefully follow all his commands and

decrees I am giving you today, all these curses will come on you and overtake you..." - Deuteronomy 28:15 (It goes on to list poverty, all physical and mental illness and many other "curses" that will befall the people of Israel if they do not observe the law)

During the days of Christ, many of the oral teachings regarding those who were ill leaned along the lines of karma. In other words, when one became ll, it was taught that their illness was caused by either their sin or their parents sin. The sickness was often treated as the righteous judgment of God against the person. As a show of righteous indignation, people would sometimes spit upon or in front of those who were ill as a way of saying they agreed with God's judgment upon the person.

"As [Jesus] passed by, He saw a man blind from birth. ² And His disciples asked Him, "Rabbi, who sinned, this man or his parents, that he would be born blind?" ³ Jesus answered, "It was neither that this man sinned, nor his parents; but it was so that the works of God might be displayed in him. ⁴ We must work the works of Him who sent Me as long as it is day; night is coming when no one can work. ⁵ While I am in the world, I am the Light of the world." ⁶ When He had said this, He spat on the ground, and made clay of the spittle, and applied the clay to his eyes, ⁷ and said to him, "Go, wash in the pool of Siloam" (which is translated, Sent). So he went away and washed, and came back seeing. - John 9:1-7

In the previous passage, what does Jesus use to heal the blind man and why would this be so deeply meaningful to the man?

"Christ redeemed us from the curse of the Law, having become a curse for us—for it is written, "Cursed is everyone who hangs on a tree"" - Galatians 3:13

According to the passage above, what did Christ do to set us free from the curse of sickness?

Another important here to make is that Jesus often healed the sick only after He pronounced their forgiveness.

"2 And they brought to Him a paralytic lying on a bed. Seeing their faith, Jesus said to the paralytic, "Take courage, son; your sins are forgiven." 3 And some of the scribes said to themselves, "This fellow blasphemes." 4 And Jesus knowing their thoughts said, "Why are you thinking evil in your hearts? 5 Which is easier, to say, 'Your sins are forgiven,' or to say, 'Get up, and walk'? 6 But so that you may know that the Son of Man has authority on earth to forgive sins"—then He *said to the paralytic, "Get up, pick up your bed and go home." 7 And he got up and went home. 8 But when the crowds saw this, they were awestruck, and glorified God, who had given such authority to men." - Matthew 9:2-8

Upon reading the passage above and understanding the curse of the law, why do you think Jesus often spoke of forgiveness of sin before He healed people?

"If you forgive the sins of any, their sins have been forgiven them; if you retain the sins of any, they have been retained." - John 20:23

What authority does Jesus give us in the passage above? What does this mean in light of the curse of the law?

RABBINIC SYNAGOGUE CULTURE

In observant Hebrew culture, the synagogue is the community center. Its the place of prayer (usually three times a day), its the place of family support, community gathering and rallying, its the place of education and schooling, and its the place of spirituality and council. A synagogue was in many ways like a spiritual community college. A place to learn and share ideas and grow in knowledge and experience.

On the sabbath days (Friday sundown through Saturday sundown) and during the weekly services, the priest wasn't the only one who ministered. It was common for the people present and even visitors to have a role in each gathering.

Today, many churches have wandered from this communal form of gathering to practice a more priest or pastor-centric gathering. Many churches have no place for a random visitor to contribute publicly in a church service. While there are definitely good reasons to have a speaker teach, it is interesting to note that most early church gatherings of the New Testament were more communal in participation and expected mutual participation.

"Jesus was going throughout all Galilee, teaching in their synagogues and proclaiming the gospel of the kingdom, and healing every kind of disease and every kind of sickness among the people." - Matthew 4:23

"When they reached Salamis, they began to proclaim the word of God in the synagogues of the Jews; and they also had John as their helper." - Acts 13:5

What do the previous two passages tell you about the structure of a synagogue and how welcoming synagogues were toward new teachers?

In the passage below, please highlight all the words or phrases that encourage the participation of multiple people in a church service.

"23 Therefore if the whole church assembles together... and all prophesy, and an unbeliever or an ungifted man enters, he is convicted by all, he is called to account by all; 25 the secrets of his heart are disclosed; and so he will fall on his face and worship God, declaring that God is certainly among you. 26 What is the outcome then, brethren? When you assemble, each one has a psalm, has a teaching, has a revelation, has a tongue, has an interpretation. Let all things be done for edification. 27 If anyone speaks in a tongue, it should be by two or at the most three, and each in turn, and one must interpret... 29 Let two or three prophets speak, and let the others pass judgment. 30 But if a revelation is made to another who is seated, the first one must keep silent. 31 For you can all prophesy

one by one, so that all may learn and all may be exhorted...." - *1 Corinthians 14:23-31*

From the days of Moses to the days of the apostles, the entire Bible is a Hebrew work. If you want to understand the New Testament in context, you must earn about rabbinic custom and culture during the first century. Jesus was a Rabbi. Without understanding some of the intricacies of the Jewish Rabbinic culture, it is nearly impossible to understand the context of a lot of the New Testament and ultimately the custom and context that Christ was revealed within.

In this chapter we have mentioned a few of the many instances where rabbinic thought and lifestyle is the context of the things said or done in the New Testament. There are also major revelations of Christ waiting to be discovered in subjects like covenant, Hebrew marriage customs, rabbinic clothing, rabbinic thought, feasts and festivals, Hebrew language and more. Some of these things will be further revealed in later chapters and books in this series but it is encouraged for each student to uncover as much as they desire on their own.

2
GOD'S PARABLES IN HEBREW PATRIARCHS

THE PURPOSE OF THE OLD TESTAMENT

The Old Testament is a record of Israel's many patriarchs, prophets and priests, scattered throughout many generations, who practiced and perceived portions of God's greater purpose in Christ. Trying to piece together the puzzle, they clung to the letter of their law and ritual, aware that their observance to these laws and repetition of these rituals was their primary link to the event those laws and rituals summoned. They were getting glimpses of the thing that would one day eclipse their activities - the Word made flesh.

God entertained the imaginations of these believers as they squinted forward, trying to comprehend the mystery of His larger picture, yet with mere shadows to work with, they had not yet come to truly know God. While the lives, laws and prophesies of the patriarchs could foreshadow Him, only an incarnate Son could fully reveal Him. Only now, with eyes wide open looking back at their lives and words through the lens of Christ, can we see and understand the brilliance of those very lives and words. Christ would come to make sense of their lives far better than they were ever able to make sense of His.

While a number of the following chapters are dedicated to extracting the fullness of God's word to us through the nation and culture of Israel, this chapter is dedicated to hearing God's word through the lives of these patriarchs. Today as much as ever, God is using their lives to speak to us.

In the space provided under each of the following passages, please explain what the passage is saying about the the Old Testament writings:

"For the Law, since it has only a shadow of the good things to come and not the very form of things, can never, by the same sacrifices which they offer continually year by year, make perfect those who draw near." - Hebrews 10:1

"...things which are a mere shadow of what is to come; but the substance belongs to Christ." - Colossians 2:17

[25] He said to them, "How foolish you are, and how slow to believe all that the prophets have spoken! [26] Did not the Messiah have to suffer these things and then enter his glory?" [27] And beginning with Moses and all the Prophets, he explained to them what was said in all the Scriptures concerning himself. - Luke 24:25-27

If you believed Moses, you would believe me, for he wrote about me. - John 5:46

[31] "He said to him, 'If they do not listen to Moses and the Prophets, they will not be convinced even if someone rises from the dead.'" - Luke 16:31

Many people ask how the God of the Old Testament and New Testament could be the same when they often act like polar opposites. There have been numerous attempts to answer this question, but few hold as much water as the Orthodox view mentioned in chapter four:

"What so many moderns find difficult is leaving behind the presumptions of either modernist Biblical Criticism or fundamentalist literalism. They are deeply married to a historical paradigm. Whereas, the paradigm of the Church is Christ Himself. He is the Alpha and the Omega, the beginning and the end. He is not judged by history but is the truth of history. There are many passages in the OT that if read literally would lead us to believe in a God far removed from the one revealed to us in Christ. This is a false reading. But many are more married to their literal historical method (of whichever form) than to Christ. Unless the OT is literal, they reason, then everything else is not true. This is not the beginning place of the Church. Truth was only ever vindicated for us in the Resurrection of Jesus Christ and that alone is our Alpha and Omega. It troubles some to begin "in the middle" though Christ resurrected is not the middle but also the beginning and the ending, if we know how to read in an Apostolic manner... Christ is risen from the dead and His resurrection becomes the center of all things. Only through His resurrection may the Old Testament be read. It's historical claims (though many are quite strong) are not the issue. Christ is the only issue and the only Truth that matters." -Orthodox minister, Fr. Stephen Freeman, "The God of the Old Testament."

GOD LIKES TO SPEAK IN PARABLES

Jesus, like many Rabbi's during His time loved to teach using parables. A parable is a didactic story used to illustrate a moral or spiritual truth. Parables often have layers of meanings and at different times can have varying applications.

¹⁰ The disciples asked him, "Why do you use stories as illustrations when you speak to people?" ¹¹ Jesus answered, "Knowledge about the mysteries of the kingdom of heaven has been given to you. But it has not been given to the crowd. ¹² Those who understand these mysteries will be given more knowledge, and they will excel in understanding them. However, some people don't understand these mysteries. Even what they understand will be taken away from them. ¹³ This is why I speak to them this way. They see, but they're blind. They hear, but they don't listen. They don't even try to understand. ¹⁴ So they make Isaiah's prophecy come true: 'You will hear clearly but never understand. You will see clearly but never comprehend.¹⁵ These people have become close-minded and hard of hearing. They have shut their eyes so that their eyes never see. Their ears never hear. Their minds never understand. And they never return to me for healing!' ¹⁶ "Blessed are your eyes because they see and your ears because they hear. ¹⁷ I can guarantee this truth: Many prophets and many of God's people longed to see what you see but didn't see it, to hear what you hear but didn't hear it. - Matthew 13:10-17 (GWV)

In the passage above, what reason did Jesus give for some people not being able to be healed by Christ's words (vs.15)?

According to this passage, why does Jesus use parables?

What does Jesus say about "many prophets and many of God's people?"

In the New Testament, we find Jesus speaking in parables but in the Old Testament, we find the patriarchs and prophets living in parables. Their lives illustrate truths about Christ and us that God uses to speak to us as we read their account in the Scriptures. In their lives God has hidden His word to us with layers of meanings and varying applications. God continues to use their lives to speak loud and clear to us to this day.

In the early church a "word of knowledge" was the gift of being able to reveal a hidden truth (logos) through the Old Testament writings and traditions. A "word of Wisdom" was the ability to apply an Old Testament story to your personal situation (rhema). The parables of Christ were considered "words of wisdom." Today, people use these terms to describe differing forms of the prophetic gift which is fine, but we should not forget what these terms were originally describing.

THE GENESIS 5 GENEALOGY

Virtually every story in the Old Testament begs us to unearth the parables, words of knowledge and words of wisdom within. In Genesis 5, we find the genealogy between Adam and Noah.

"This is the book of the generations of Adam. In the day when God created man, He made him in the likeness of God. ² He created them male and female, and He blessed them and named them Man in the day when they were created. ³ When Adam had lived one hundred and thirty years, he became the father of a son in his own likeness, according to his image, and named him Seth.

4 Then the days of Adam after he became the father of Seth were eight hundred years, and he had other sons and daughters. 5 So all the days that Adam lived were nine hundred and thirty years, and he died. 6 Seth lived one hundred and five years, and became the father of Enosh..." [it goes on to give the rest of the Genealogy until Noah] - Genesis 5:1-32

If we translate the genealogy from Adam to Noah found in Genesis 5 in order, we find something quite amazing!

NAME with HEBREW NAME MEANING	
Adam	= Man
Seth	= Appointed
Enosh	= Mortal
Kenan	= Dwelling
Mahelalel	= The Almighty God
Jared	= Shall come down (or Descend)
Enoch	= Teaching
Methusalah	= His Death Shall Bring
Lamech	= The Despairing
Noah	= Rest and Comfort

Together, this genealogy reads: "Man (was) appointed (a) mortal dwelling, (but) the Almighty

God shal come down teaching, His death shall bring the despairing rest and comfort. - The gospel was already being preached in the Genesis 5 genealogy account.

As we move forward, we will go through an abbreviated list of the major patriarchs (Adam, Noah, Abraham, Joseph, Moses and David) and their parallel with Christ. Feel free to turn each of of these into a deeper Bible Study. Seeing the riches we mine from these patriarchs will hopefully inspire you to search out the rest of the Old Testament parables (peoples) in search of more treasure.

ADAM AS A TYPE OF CHRIST

In the space provided under each of the following passages, please describe how the following passages compare Adam to Christ:

...Adam, who is a type of Him who was to come. - Romans 5:14

"If there is a natural body, there is also a spiritual body. ^{45} So also it is written, "The first man, Adam, became a living soul." The last Adam (Christ) became a life-giving spirit. ^{46}However, the spiritual is not first, but the natural; then the spiritual. ^{47} The first man is from the earth, earthy; the second man is from heaven..." - 1 Corinthians 15:44-47

We read in these and other Scriptures that Adam is a type of Christ. The primary point of the Old Testament was to point to Christ. When Christ was revealed, it was as if He offered a job evaluation of the Old Covenant.

"For if that first covenant had been faultless, there would have been no occasion sought for a second.⁸ For finding fault with them, He (God) says, "Behold, days are coming, says the Lord, When I will effect a new covenant..." - Hebrews 8:7-8

There have been many debates, especially in the first three centuries of Church history, about how much of the Old Covenant (if any) we should continue to observe. Many of these early debates were fierce with some arguing that there was no way to reconcile the God of Moses and the God of Jesus, and others saying that it was the same God, but we were beholding Him through the lens of two differing covenants. Whatever the case, both sides can agree that the point of the Old Testament was to point to Christ. And when looking for doctrine, and for an accurate picture of God, Christ trumps all. Differences between the Old and New Testaments should't be emphasized to the point of conflict. That being said, the old and the new are both undoubtedly the product of the same divine mind. This is more than evident in the connection between Adam and Christ.

Below you will find a few of the Old Testament passages that deal with Adam. Each one offers a detail or two that can be compared or contrasted with Christ. Please note how each New Testament passage reveals Christ as the fulfillment of the Old Testament Adam.

IMAGE & LIKENESS:
O.T. - *"Then God said, "Let Us make man in Our image, according to Our likeness... ^{27} God created man in His own image, in the image of God He created him..." - Genesis 1:26-27*

N.T. - *"[Jesus] is the image of the invisible God, the firstborn of all creation." - Colossians 1:15*

AUTHORITY & DOMINION:
O.T. - *"Then God said... 'let them have dominion over the fish of the sea, over the birds of the air, and over the cattle, over all[b] the earth and over every creeping thing that creeps on the earth." - Genesis 1:26-27*

N.T. - *"For He has put all things in subjection under His feet. But when He says, "All things are put in subjection," it is evident that He is excepted who put all things in subjection to Him." - 1 Corinthians 15:27*

N.T. - *"^{20} which He brought about in Christ, when He raised Him from the dead and seated Him at His right hanc in the heavenly places, ^{21} far above all rule and authority and power and dominion, and every name that is named, not only in this age but also in the one to come. ^{22} And He put all things in subjection under His feet, and gave Him as head over all things to the church..." - Ephesians 1:20-22*

SIDE OPENED, PRODUCES BRIDE:
O.T. - *"And the Lord God caused a deep sleep to fall on Adam, and he slept; and He took one of his ribs, and closed up the flesh in its place. ^{22} Then the rib which the Lord God had taken from man He*

made into a woman, and He brought her to the man. - Genesis 2:21-22

N.T. - *"But one of the soldiers pierced His side with a spear, and immediately blood and water came out." - John 19:34*

N.T. - *"Husbands, love your wives, just as Christ also loved the church and gave Himself up for her, [26] so that He might sanctify her, having cleansed her by the washing of water with the word, [27] that He might present to Himself the church in all her glory, having no spot or wrinkle or any such thing; but that she would be holy and blameless." - Ephesians 5:25-27*

As we can begin to see from the examples above, there are many parallels between the life of Adam and the life of Christ. Every disciple of Christ will benefit greatly from regularly meditating on the life of Adam. Below you will find a short list of other parallels between the life of Adam and the life of Christ.

- *Adam came out of a virgin earth, Christ came out of a virgin Mary.*
- *The first Adam turned from the Father in the garden of Eden; the last Adam turned to the Father in the garden of Gethsemane.*
- *The first Adam was naked & unashamed in the garden; the last Adam was naked & bore our shame on the cross.*
- *The first Adam's sin brought us thorns; the last Adam wore a crown of thorns.*
- *The first Adam sinned at a tree; the last Adam bore our sins on a tree.*
- *The first Adam died as a sinner; the last Adam died for sinners.*
- *The first Adam lost the tree of life; the last Adam is the tree of life.*

- *The first Adam was the head of the old creation; the last Adam is the head of the new creation.*
- *The first Adam was created in God's image; the last Adam is God's exact image.*
- *The first Adam was seeking a wife; the last Adam is seeking a wife.*
- *The first Adam was put to sleep to produce Eve; the last Adam was put to death to produce the church.*
- *The first Adam named woman; the last Adam names each one of us with new names*
- *The first Adam came out from the ground; the last Adam fell into the ground.*
- *The first Adam became a living soul; the last Adam became a life-giving Spirit.*
- *The first Adam's side was opened; the last Adam's side was opened.*
- *Eve was taken out of the first Adam; the church was taken out of the last Adam.*
- *Eve was brought to the first Adam without sin; the church will be presented to the last Adam without sin.*
- *Eve was the same as the first Adam in life, nature, & expression; the church is the same as the last Adam in life, nature, & expression.*
- *The first Adam & Eve became one flesh; the last Adam & the church have become one spirit.*

We have looked at the ways Adam was a "type" of Christ, but he is also a type of you! Do you know what it is to walk in naked innocence before God? Have you ever felt shame or fear from having sinned against God? Have you ever felt a slave to anything? There are so many ways in which Adam's life story can apply to you.

Read through the story of Adam. In the space below, please note some of the words of knowledge (theology) or words of wisdom (rhema) you get from Adam's life that pertain to you.

NOAH AS A TYPE OF CHRIST

The similarities between Noah and Jesus are also astonishing! So much so that we may affirm the ark to be a symbolic representation of what Jesus would later do for us on the cross of Calvary.

In the space provided under the following passage, please describe how it relates Noah to Christ:

[37] For the coming of the Son of Man will be just like the days of Noah. [38] For as in those days before the flood they were eating and drinking, marrying and giving in marriage, until the day that Noah entered the ark, [39] and they did not understand until the flood came and took them all away; so will the coming of the Son of Man be. - Matthew 24:37-39

Below you will find a few of the Old Testament passages that deal with Noah. Each one offers a detail or two that can be compared or contrasted with Christ. Please note how each New Testament passage reveals Christ as the fulfillment of the Old Testament Noah.

UNCORRUPTED IN HIS GENERATION:

OT - "Then the Lord saw that the wickedness of man was great on the earth, and that every intent of the thoughts of his heart was only evil continually... [6] The Lord ...was grieved in His heart. [7] The Lord said, "... I am sorry that I have made them."[8] But Noah found favor in the eyes of the Lord. [9] Noah was a righteous man, blameless in his time." - Genesis 6:5-9

NT - "He made Him who knew no sin *to be* sin on our behalf, so that we might become the righteousness of God in Him." - 2 Corinthians 5:21

NT - "For it was fitting for us to have such a high priest, holy, innocent, undefiled, separated from sinners and exalted above the heavens." - Hebrews 7:26

WALKED WITH GOD:

OT - "Noah walked with God." - Genesis 6:9

NT - And Jesus kept increasing in wisdom and stature, and in favor with God and men." - Luke 2:52,

"It was at this time that He went off to the mountain to pray, and He spent the whole night in prayer to God." - 6:12

A COVENANT WITH YOU AND YOURS:

OT - "But I will establish My covenant with you; and you shall enter the ark—you and your sons and your wife, and your sons' wives with you." - Genesis 6:18

NT - "Now the God of peace, who brought up from the dead the great Shepherd of the sheep through the blood of the eternal covenant, *even* Jesus our Lord." - Hebrews 13:20

NT - [6] "I have manifested Your name to the men whom You gave Me out of the world; they were Yours and You gave them to Me, and they have kept Your word. [7] Now they have come to know *that everything You have given Me is from You;* ⁸ *for the words which You gave Me I have given to them; and they received them and truly understood that I came forth from You, and they believed that You sent Me.* ⁹ *I ask on their behalf; I do not ask on behalf of the world, but of those whom You have given Me; for they are Yours;* ¹⁰ *and all things that are Mine are Yours, and Yours are Mine; and I have been glorified in them.* ¹¹ *I am no longer in the world; and yet they themselves are in the world, and I come to You. Holy Father, keep them in Your name, the name which You have given Me, that they may be one even as We are.* ¹² *While I was with them, I was keeping them in Your name which You have given Me; and I guarded them and not one of them perished..."* - John 17:6-26

As we can begin to see from the examples above, there are many parallels between the life of Noah and the life of Christ. Below you will find a short list of other parallels between the life of Adam and the life of Christ.

- The Ark was covered both inside and out with "pitch." The Hebrew word for 'pitch' is 'kaphar' and it is used seventy times in the Bible to mean atonement as it relates to blood sacrifice. The one exception is here in Genesis where it refers to the tar-like substance which covers the ark inside-and-out.
- In Noah's ark, Mankind was saved from destruction. The Cross of Christ is the ark of man's salvation. In it, mankind was saved from destruction.
- In noah's Ark, mankind ascended far above the mountains into the heavens. In Christ, mankind ascends far above the mountains into the heavens.
- Ark was God's plan of salvation, revealed in advance. Christ was God's plan of salvation revealed in advance.

- *In the Ark, both Lion and Lamb, predators and prey all laid down together in harmony. In Christ, all of Creation comes into union and harmony.*
- *Ark only had one Door, Christ is the door. (Gen. 6:16) (John 10:9; 14:6)*
- *Ark only had one window (In the ceiling), revealing the direction of Christ's vision.*
- *Ark was a shelter from the storm. Christ calmed the storm.*
- *Noah means, rest and comfort, Holy Spirit, is rest and comfort.*
- *Noah went to prepare a place for them. Christ goes to prepare a place for us.*
- *In Noah's ark, there were many dwelling places, In our Fathers house, Christ says there are many dwelling places.*
- *God flooded the world with rain, God flooded the world with the Spirit.*
- *The rain of Noah brought death, the rain of Christ brings life.*
- *In Noah, the world was sacrificed as a strategy against sin, in Christ, the begotten of God was sacrificed as a strategy against sin.*
- *Upon Noah, the Dove ascended as a sign of peace and favor, upon Christ, the dove ascended as a sign of peace and favor.*
- *To many of the people of Noah's day, the ark was foolishness. To the people of Jesus' day, the cross was foolishness.*
- *In Noah's Ark, they were all sealed and secure, In the Holy Spirit sent by Christ we are all sealed and secure.*
- *When Noah finished his work, mankind entered in and was saved, not because of their own labors but by his. When Christ finished His work, mankind entered in and was saved, not as a result of their own works, but by His alone.*
- *Earth Purified of all wickedness in Noah, Earth purified of all wickedness in Christ.*
- *With Noah, The earth received water from heaven for 40 days and 40 nights. With Christ, fasted 40 days 40 nights. and in the Resurrection, Christ appeared for 40 days, 40 nights.*

As you can see, Noah is a "type" of Christ. He is also a type of you! Have you ever felt like you are the only moral person in the crowd? Has God ever called you to a project that takes many years to complete? Have you ever felt responsible to save people from their destruction? Have you ever felt so favored by God that He would choose you for some special task? There are so many ways in which Noah's life story can apply to you!

Read through the story of Noah. In the space below, please note some of the words of knowledge (theology) or words of wisdom (rhema) you get from Noah's life that pertain to you.

ABRAHAM AS A TYPE OF FATHER GOD

In the space provided under each of the following passages, please describe what the passages say about God's relation to you.

"There is one God and Father of all who is over all and through all and in all." - Ephesians 4:6,

"Do not call anyone on earth your father; for One is your Father, He who is in heaven." - Matthew 23:9,

" Yet for us there is but one God, the Father, from whom are all things and we exist for Him; and one Lord, Jesus Christ, by whom are all things, and we exist through Him." - 1 Corinthians 8:6

As you can see from the passages above, God is the true Father of us all. The scriptures also tell us that Abraham is our father. Many people have a hard time reconciling the seemingly contrary statements in the Bible. When we step back and see that the point of the Old Testament wasn't primarily to relay natural facts (although it does) as it was to convey spiritual truth, it becomes a lot easier to appreciate and learn from the Old Testament.

In the space provided under the following passage, please describe what is revealed about Abraham's relation to you.

Rom 4:16-17 'Therefore, the promise comes by faith, so that it may be by grace and may be guaranteed to all Abraham's offspring—not only to those who are of the law but also to those who are of the faith of Abraham. He is the father of us all. As it is written: "I have made you a father of many nations." He is our father in the sight of God, in whom he believed —the God who gives life to the dead and calls things that are not as though they were.'

As we can begin to see from the examples above, there are many parallels between the life of Abraham and God. Below you will find a short list of other parallels.

- *Abraham is the Father of Multitudes, God is the father of multitudes.*
- *Abraham has two sons of promise, Ishmael and Isaac. God has two sons of promise, Adam and Jesus.*
- *Abraham's first born son, Ishmael, with his descendants, were born into slavery, God's firstborn son, Adam, with his descendants, were born into slavery.*

- *Abraham's second born son, Isaac, with his descendants, were born into favor and abundance, God's second born son, Jesus, with his descendants, were born into favor and abundance.*
- *Abraham had two sons whom he loved, one slave and one free. God has two types of sons whom He loves, one who is still acting a slave to sin and one who has been set free.*
- *Abrahams first born was born according to the flesh and second according to the Spirit, God's firstborn was in the flesh, second was in the Spirit. (Galatians 4:28)*
- *Abraham has many descendants of the flesh, but not of the spirit. God has many children of the flesh, but not of the Spirit.*
- *The son born according to the flesh is sent away from Abraham's presence, but his kingdom is given to the son born according to the Spirit. The son born according to the flesh is sent away from God's presence, the garden of Eden, but his kingdom is given to the son born according to the Spirit, Christ.*
- *Abraham is distressed that Ishmael is sent away. God is distressed that Adam is sent away.*
- *The Slave woman's son, (Ishmael) cannot share in the inheritance of Abraham. The Slave woman's son, (Adam) cannot share in the inheritance of God.*
- *Abraham was set to sacrifice his son. God was set to sacrifice His son.*
- *Abraham had Isaac carry the wood that he would be sacrificed on, Christ carried the wood that he would be sacrificed on.*
- *Isaac was unsure about the intent of his father Abraham in the sacrifice, Christ questioned His Father in the sacrifice.*
- *Abraham desired a wife for his son Isaac so he sends an unnamed servant to find her. God desires a wife for his Son Jesus so he sends the Holy Spirit to gather her.*

As you can see, Abraham is a "type" of Father God. That being said, Abraham is also a type of you! Has God ever called you to a place you've never been before? Has God ever promised you

the impossible and then stalled in making it come to pass? Have you ever been called to be a spiritual or natural leader or parent? There are so many ways in which Abraham's life story can apply to you!

Read through the story of Abraham. In the space below, please note some of the words of knowledge (theology) or words of wisdom (rhema) you get from Abraham's life that pertain to you.

JOSEPH AS A TYPE OF CHRIST

If any story in the Old Testament foreshadowed Jesus, it was Joseph, the son of Jacob (Israel).

In the space provided under each of the following passages, please describe how the following passages relate Joseph to Christ:

"Now Israel loved Joseph more than all his sons, because he was the son of his old age; and he made him a varicolored tunic. ⁴ His brothers saw that their father loved him more than all his brothers; and so they hated him and could not speak to him on friendly terms." - Genesis 37:3-5 (To answer, see Matthew 3:17, 12:18, John 7:3-5 & 15:18-19)

"Then Pharaoh said to his servants, "Can we find a man like this, in whom is a divine spirit?" ³⁹ So Pharaoh said to Joseph, "Since God has informed you of all this, there is no one so discerning and wise

as you are. ⁴⁰ You shall be over my house, and according to your command all my people shall do homage; only in the throne I will be greater than you." ⁴¹ Pharaoh said to Joseph, "See, I have set you over all the land of Egypt." ⁴² Then Pharaoh took off his signet ring from his hand and put it on Joseph's hand, and clothed him in garments of fine linen and put the gold necklace around his neck. ⁴³ He had him ride in his second chariot; and they proclaimed before him, "Bow the knee!" And he set him over all the land of Egypt." - Genesis 41:38-43 (To answer, see Luke 4:1, Acts 2:32-33, & Philippians 2:10)

As we can begin to see from the examples above, there are many parallels between the life of Joseph and Jesus. Below you will find a short list of other parallels.

- *Joseph was firstborn, Jesus was firstborn (Gen 30:22-24 of Rachel, Mt. 1:25 of Mary)*
- *Both were saviors and given a name meaning Savior. (Gen 41:45 & 47:25, Mat 1:21 & Acts 13:23*
- *Joseph was a Shepherd, Jesus is the Great Shepherd Gen 37:2 John 10-11*
- *Joseph was 30 years old when he began his Ministry, Jesus was 30 years when He started His Gen 41:46, Luke 3:23*
- *Joseph was "beloved" of his father, Jesus was beloved of His Father*
- *Joseph was prophesied to be a ruler, Christ was prophesied to be a ruler (Gen.37:5-11, Dan. 7:13-14, Micah 4:7,5:2)*
- *Joseph was sent unto his brethren, Jesus was sent to His brethren, the lost sheep of Israel (Gen 37:13,18-20, Mt. 21:37-38)*
- *Joseph's brethren refused to receive him, Jesus' brethren refused to receive Him.*

- *Joseph was sold as a slave by his brethren, Jesus was sold for the price of a slave (Gen 37:27-28, Matt 26:15*
- *Joseph was unjustly accused and condemned, so was Jesus Gen 39:13-14,*
- *Joseph and Jesus were silent before their accusers Gen 39:20, Mark 15:4*
- *Joseph was buried in prison, so was Jesus in the Tomb of Joseph*
- *Both were with two others condemned to die, one of which was pardoned and given life. Gen 40:1-3, 20-22, Luke 23:32,39-43)*
- *Joseph was resurrected from prison and exalted to sit with Pharoah on his throne, so Jesus was resurrected and exalted to sit on His Father's Throne.*
- *Joseph went to Egypt, Jesus went to Egypt. (Gen 37:28, Mt. 2:13-15)*
- *God's Spirit indwelt Joseph, God's Spirit indwelt Jesus. (Gen 41:38, Luke 4:1, Acts 10:38)*
- *Joseph on the throne became the dispenser of bread to starving Egypt, so Jesus on His Father's Throne is the "Bread of Life" for a perishing world. Gen 41:57.*
- *The king of Egypt appointed Joseph to be the sole source of life for all. God appointed Jesus to be our sole source of eternal life. (Gen. 41:55-57, Acts 4:12, 1 John 5:11-12)*
- *The king of Egypt exalted Joseph ruler over all to bring all under the king's rule. Jesus is exalted to bring all under God's rule. (Gen 41:40-44, Acts 2:32-33, 1 Cor 15:27-28)*
- *Joseph knew his brethren the first time, but they did not know him, so Jesus knew His brethren when He came the first time but they knew him not. (Gen 42:7-8)*
- *Joseph made himself known to his brethren when they came the "Second time", so Jesus will be recognized by the Jews when He comes the Second Time. (Gen 45:3-4)*
- *After Joseph was exalted he got Asenath, - a Gentile Bride, so Jesus is receiving a Gentile Bride after his resurrection – The Church. (Gen 41:45, 2 Cor 11:2)*
- *After Joseph received his (gentile) bride, his brethren then suffered a seven year famine and they came to him for food,*

> Likewise, after Jesus gets His Bride, the scriptures prophesy the world will see a 7 year period of tribulation. (Gen 41:54, Mat 23:21-22, Rev 7:14)
> - The evil Joseph's brothers intended God meant for good to save them. The same is true of the evil Jesus' own people intended to him... (Gen 45:5-8, 50:20, Acts 3:12-18)
> - Joseph's brothers shared Pharaoh's favor because of Joseph, not themselves. We share God's favor because of Jesus, not because we are worthy. (Gen 45:16-20, Eph 2:4-8, Phil 4:19)

As you can see, Joseph is a "type" of Christ. And just like all the others, Joseph is also a type of you! Have you ever been unjustly accused? Have you ever felt like you were forgotten in a prison for years? Have you been rejected by those closest to you and even been conspired against? Have you tried to act in righteousness only for it to backfire on you? Has God promised you something and it taken a long, long time to come? Have you ever been saved and rewarded by God with overwhelming abundance? There are so many ways in which Joseph's life story might speak to you!

Read through the story of Joseph. In the space below, please note some of the words of knowledge (theology) or words of wisdom (rhema) you get from Joseph's life that pertain to you.

MOSES AS A TYPE OF CHRIST

Moses is also such a revealing type of Christ. Please note how the New Testament passages below reveal Christ as the fulfillment of the Old

Testament passage of Moses.

KINGS SOUGHT THEIR DEATH AT BIRTH

OT - "Then Pharaoh commanded all his people, saying, 'Every son who is born you are to cast into the Nile, and every daughter you are to keep alive.' - Exodus 1:22

NT - "Then when Herod saw that he had been tricked by the magi, he became very enraged, and sent and slew all the male children who were in Bethlehem and all its vicinity, from two years old and under, according to the time which he had determined from the magi." - Matthew 2:16

As we can begin to see from the examples above, there are many parallels between the life of Moses and Jesus. Below you will find a short list of other parallels.

- *Moses was an Israelite (Ex. 2:1, 2). Jesus was also an Israelite according to the flesh.*
- *Moses was born while his people were under the rule of a hostile nation (Egypt), Jesus was born while his people were under the rule of a hostile nation (Rome). (Ex. 1, Matthew 2:1 cf. Luke 24: 21)*
- *Moses' life was preserved through adoption by Pharaoh's daughter, Jesus' life was preserved through adoption by Joseph. (Ex. 2:10, Matt 1:19-21)*
- *Moses childhood was spent in Egypt, Jesus childhood was spent in Egypt. (Matt 2:13, Hosea 11:1)*
- *Moses had compassion for his people Israel, Jesus had compassion for His people Israel. (Acts 7:23, 24)*
- *Moses was not ashamed to call the Hebrew slaves his brethren, Jesus was not ashamed to call us His brethren. (Ex. 2:11, Heb. 2:11)*

- *Pharoah made himself of no reputation, Jesus made himself of no reputation. (Heb. 11:24-26, Phil. 2:6, 7)*
- *Moses was rejected by his brethren, Jesus was rejected by his brethren. (Acts 7:26, 27, John 1:11)*
- *Moses dwelt in the land of Gentiles (Midian), Jesus dwelt in Galilee of the Gentiles. (Ex. 2:15, Acts 15:14)*
- *Moses was a shepherd, Jesus was the great Shepherd. (Ex. 3:1, John 10:16).*
- *Moses spent many years in obscurity before his mission, Jesus spent many years in obscurity before his mission.*
- *Moses was personally called by God to emancipate His people from the house of bondage, Jesus was personally called by God to emancipate His people from the house of bondage (Ex. 3:10, Luke 19:10).*
- *Moses' commission from God was confirmed by miracles, signs and wonders, Jesus' commission from God was confirmed by miracles, signs and wonders. (Matthew 11:4, 5)*
- *Moses' first two miraculous signs were power over the serpent, and power over leprosy, Jesus' first two miraculous signs were power over the serpent, and power over leprosy. (Ex. 4:6-9, Matt 4:10, 11, 8:3)*
- *Moses returned after fleeing to his hometown, Jesus returned after fleeing to his hometown. (Ex 4:19, Matt 2:19)*
- *Moses wielded a rod of mighty power, Jesus wields a rod of mighty power. (Ex 9:23; 10:13; 14:16. Ps. 2:9).*
- *Moses called Pharoah to repentance, Jesus calls His people to repentance. (Luke 13:3).*
- *Moses set Israel free from bondage, Jesus set Israel free from bondage. (Acts 7:35, John 8:36).*
- *Israel was said to have been baptized into Moses, New Covenant believers are called to be baptized into Christ. (1 Cor. 10:1, 2, Rom. 6:3).*
- *Moses' authority was challenged, Jesus' authority was challenged. (Num 16:3, Matt 21:23)*
- *Those who Moses served murmured against him, those who Jesus served murmured against Him. (Ex 15:24, 16:2, Luke 15:2, John 6:41)*

- *The Hebrews sought to stone Moses, the Hebrews sought to stone Jesus. (Ex. 17:4, John 8:59, 10:31)*
- *Moses always was found praying, Jesus was always praying. (Exodus 5:22, 8:12, 9:33, 14:15, 15:25, 17:4)*
- *Moses was called meek, Jesus was called meek (Num. 12:3, Matt 11:29)*
- *Moses turned water to blood, Jesus turned water to wine.*
- *Moses called a priest, Jesus called our priest. (Ps. 99:6, Lev 8:15-16, Heb. 9:14).*
- *Moses ruled as a king, Jesus rules as a King. (Deut. 33:4-5, Luke 1:32-33).*
- *Moses sat the judge of the Israelites, Jesus has been given all judgment. (Ex. 18:13, 2 Cor 5:10)*
- *Moses stood as mediator between God and man, Jesus stands as mediator between God and man.(Deut. 5:5, 1 Tim. 2:5).*
- *Moses was used to heal people by having them look at a bronze serpent on a cross, Jesus healed people by becoming their sin upon a cross!*
- *Moses was the receptacle of God's covenant with Israel, Jesus is the receptacle of God's covenant with us. (Ex. 34:27, Heb. 8:6).*
- *Moses chose and sent out twelve, Jesus chose and sent out twelve. (Num. 13:16, Matt 10:5)*
- *Moses appointed seventy, Jesus appointed seventy. (Num. 11:24, Luke 10:1)*
- *Moses knew the Lord face to face, Jesus knew God face to face. (Ex. 34:10, John 1:18).*
- *Moses delivered God's commandments, Jesus delivered God's commandments. (Deut 4:2, Matt 28:20)*
- *Moses fasted 40 days and nights, Jesus fasted 40 days and nights. (Ex 34:28, Matt 4:2)*
- *Moses was transfigured on the mount, Jesus was transfigured on the mount. (Ex 34:29, 35, Matt 17:2)*
- *Moses prayed for Israel's forgiveness. Jesus prayed for Israel's forgiveness. (Num 14:19, Luke 23:34)*
- *Moses washed his brethren with water, Jesus washes his brethren with water. (Lev. 8:6)*

- *Moses did according to all that the Lord commanded, Jesus did according to all that God commanded, (Ex. 40:16, John 16:10)*
- *Moses built a tabernacle of God's presence, Jesus was the tabernacle of God's presence. (Ex 40:2, Zech 6:12)*
- *Moses anointed God's house, Jesus anoints God's house -us! (Lev. 8:10, Acts 2:1-3, 33)*
- *Moses' life and death benefitted the people, Jesus' life and death benefitted the people. (Ps. 106:32, Deut. 3:26).*
- *Moses appointed a comforter to take his place, Jesus appointed a comforter to take His place. (Deut 31:23, John 14:16-18)*

As you can see, Moses is a "type" of Christ. And just like all the others, Moses is also a type of you! Have you ever been called to stand up to injustice? Have you ever had to lead a group of people who don't totally trust your leadership? Have you ever been faced with impossible situations, only to have God provide a way for you? Have you ever been nervous when called to deliver a message for God? There are so many ways in which Moses' life story might speak to you!

Read through the story of Moses. In the space below, please note some of the words of knowledge (theology) or words of wisdom (rhema) you get from Moses' life pertaining to you.

DAVID AS A TYPE OF CHRIST

David is also such a revealing type of Christ. In the space provided under each of the following passages, please describe how the following passages relate David to Christ:

"Now in the sixth month the angel Gabriel was sent from God to a city in Galilee called Nazareth, 27 to a virgin engaged to a man whose name was Joseph, of the descendants of David; and the virgin's name was Mary. 28 And coming in, he said to her, "Greetings, favored one! The Lord is with you." 29 But she was very perplexed at this statement, and kept pondering what kind of salutation this was. 30 The angel said to her, "Do not be afraid, Mary; for you have found favor with God. 31 And behold, you will conceive in your womb and bear a son, and you shall name Him Jesus. 32 He will be great and will be called the Son of the Most High; and the Lord God will give Him the throne of His father David; 33 and He will reign over the house of Jacob forever, and His kingdom will have no end." - Luke 1:26-33

"As Jesus went on from there, two blind men followed Him, crying out, "Have mercy on us, Son of David!" 28 When He entered the house, the blind men came up to Him, and Jesus *said to them, "Do you believe that I am able to do this?" They *said to Him, "Yes, Lord." 29 Then He touched their eyes, saying, "It shall be done to you according to your faith." - Matthew 9:27-29

Seventeen verses in the New Testament label Jesus as the son of David. During the days of the incarnation of Christ, the jewish people had all been taught that the Messiah would come from the line of David (Psalm 132:11, Isaiah 9:7, Jer. 32:4-5, etc...).

When the people came with requests, labeling Jesus "the son of David," they were acknowledging Him as Messiah and affirming faith in what He could therefor do.

As we can begin to see from the examples above, there are many parallels between the life of David and Jesus. Below you will find a short list of other parallels.

- *David born in Bethlehem, Jesus born in Bethlehem (1 Sam. 17:12)*
- *David's name means "beloved," Jesus is called beloved. (?)*
- *David was a shepherd, Jesus is called the Great Shepherd.*
- *Goliath taunted Israel for forty days before David defeated him, Jesus was tempted by the devil for forty days before defeating him. (1 Sam 17:16,*
- *David was sent from his father to the battle, Jesus was sent from His Father to the battle. (1 Sam 17:17-18, 1 John 4:14)*
- *David was accused and rejected by his brothers, Jesus was accused and rejected by his brothers. (1 Sam 17:28, John 7:5)*
- *David learned obedience from suffering, Jesus learned obedience from suffering. (1 Sam 17:33-37, Heb. 5:8)*
- *David was chosen to fight Goliath as the "soul representative" of all of Israel, which meant his defeat or victory was Israel's defeat or victory regardless of their participation. Jesus was chosen as the "soul representative" of all of mankind, which means victory was our victory regardless of our participation. (1 Pet 3:18, Heb 10:10)*
- *David defeated Goliath who's name means "Nakedness & Exile," Jesus defeated the "nakedness and exile" that Adam and Eve brought to us all in the Garden. (Rom 5:18-19)*
- *David defeated the chief warrior of the Philistines and all the other philistines then fled before Israel, Jesus defeated the chief of the devils, Satan, and all the other devils now flee before us. (1 Sam 17:51-53, Rom 5:19)*
- *David disarmed Goliath, Jesus disarmed the rulers and principalities (Col 2;15*

- *David cut off Goliath's head just outside the walls of Jerusalem on a hill which became known as "Golgotha," which means "the place of the [Goliath's] skull." Jesus was crucified on this very hill, signifying the purpose and victory of His death.*
- *David was made the King of the Jews, Jesus is the King of the Jews.*
- *David was friends with the distressed, indebted and discontented, Jesus was friends with the sinners and tax collectors. (1 Sam 22:1-2,*
- *David was despised by His own bride, the scriptures warn us that some in the Church will fall away and despise Christ. (2 Samuel 6:16,*

As you can see, David is a "type" of Christ. And just like all the others, David is also a type of you! Do you love to sing to God? Have you ever felt righteous anger? Have you ever had to rule over others? Have you ever been displaced by someone you love? Have others ever contended greedily with you over what is yours? There are so many ways in which David's life story might speak to you!

Read through the story of David. In the space below, please note some of the words of knowledge (theology) or words of wisdom (rhema) you get from his life pertaining to you.

In this chapter we have merely begun to open the door to the parables and wisdom God has given us in the Old Testament patriarchs. We have not even touched on the lives of Sarah, Samuel, Elijah, Elisha, Isaiah, Esther, Jeremiah, Ezekiel, Daniel, Hosea and so many others. The entire Old Testament is filled with shadows and types of Christ and they are all shadows and types that can and often do speak of you too. God has and will continue to use the stories of the Old Testament to speak to us personally about our lives.

3

THE ANCIENT HEBREW CONCEPT OF COVENANT

INTRODUCTION TO COVENANT

Many believers today have little or no concept of covenant yet the entire Bible was written in context to covenant. Every word in the Bible is a covenant word! Before He ever begins to relate to us, or dispense any benefits to us, He always creates a covenant to establish the parameters and worth of that relationship.

The word "covenant" occurs 292 times in the Bible. Throughout the scriptures God chooses to use the term "covenant" to describe how He relates to His people. Covenant is a type of relationship. It is the only type of relationship God is willing to enter into. Covenant is Gods exclusive style of relationship with us. From Genesis to Revelation, God never operates with man outside of the context of covenant.

"All the paths of the Lord are lovingkindness and truth to those who keep His covenant and His testimonies." - Psalm 25:10

What does Psalm 25:10 say about those who keep God's covenant and His testimonies?

COVENANT IN ANCIENT CULTURE

The entire Bible was written in context to covenant. Ancient society was based on covenant. For this reason, all blessing and progress in God is through our participation in covenant. Once you understand covenant, you can understand the Bible and the God of the Bible. Until you understand covenant, it is nearly impossible to understand much of the Bible or the God of the Bible. God is a covenant making and a covenant keeping God!

In the days of Abraham, often, two families would want to covenant together for the sake of security or provision. They would say, "we will be better off doing this together than separate." So, they would cut a covenant. This would mean that their families were bound together for up to 10 generations! To cut a covenant, they would bring five animals together, a heifer, a goat, a ram, a turtledove, and a young pigeon and they would cut them down the spine and with both families facing eachother the two heads of the houses would stand in the blood and exchange vows, weapons, names and mantles. They would say, "If I break this covenant, may the women in my tribe never produce a child again and may my crops never produce a harvest again." They would then eat a meal together and the covenant would be sealed! Covenants were said to be even stronger than family and so if your own brother became the enemy of your covenant partner, you would have to side with your covenant partner.

"A man of too many friends comes to ruin, but there is a friend who sticks closer than a brother." - Proverbs 18:24

What does Proverbs 18:24 say about the strength of covenant ties verses the strenght of family ties?

In 1 Samuel 20, we find the famous story of David, Jonathan and Jonathan's father, King Saul. In the story, Saul has secretly become jealous of David and is seeking to kill him while Jonathan and

David's friendship becomes so deep they decide to cut a covenant.

"*^{12} Then Jonathan said to David, 'The Lord, the God of Israel, be witness!' ^{16} ...So Jonathan made a covenant with the house of David, saying, 'May the Lord require it at the hands of David's enemies.' ^{17} Jonathan made David vow again because of his love for him, because he loved him as he loved his own life...*" 1 Samuel 20:12-17

As you can see from the passage above, Jonathan and David were cutting a covenant. Shortly after the covenant is cut, David learns of Saul's desire to kill him and questions Jonathan about Sauls intentions. Jonathan doubts David's accusations, but then realizes it is true. Jonathan then begins to help David hide from Saul. Upon realizing that Jonathan is helping David, Saul becomes furious.

"*^{30} Then Saul's anger burned against Jonathan and he said to him, "You son of a perverse, rebellious woman! Do I not know that you are choosing the son of Jesse to your own shame and to the shame of your mother's nakedness? ^{31} For as long as the son of Jesse lives on the earth, neither you nor your kingdom will be established. Therefore now, send and bring him to me, for he must surely die." ^{32} But Jonathan answered Saul his father and said to him, 'Why should he be put to death? What has he done?' ^{33} Then Saul hurled his spear at him to strike him down: so Jonathan knew that his father had decided to put David to death. ^{34} Then Jonathan arose from the table in fierce anger, and did not eat food on the second day of the new moon, for he was grieved over David because his father had dishonored him... ^{42} Jonathan said to David, "Go in* *safety, inasmuch as we have sworn to each other in the name of the Lord, saying, 'The Lord will be between me and you, and between my descendants and your descendants forever.' Then he rose and departed, while Jonathan went into the city." - 1 Samuel 20:12-42*

In the passage above, what was Sauls response and how was Jonathans covenant put to the test?

[51] Do you suppose that I came to grant peace on earth? I tell you, no, but rather division; [52] for from now on five members in one household will be divided, three against two and two against three. [53] They will be divided, father against son and son against father, mother against daughter and daughter against mother, mother-in-law against daughter-in-law and daughter-in-law against mother-in-law." - Luke 12:51-53

In the passage above, Jesus is using covenant words. What is He saying?

Kay Arthur in her book, "Our covenant God" wrote of the language of the culture of the Old Testament concerning covenant. This is what "Covenant" meant within the context and culture of the Bible.

"The animals had been slain cut in half down the spine, their bright blood stained the stones the dirt and the grass in its display of color. -A covenant was being cut. The two men stood opposite of each other, each removed his own robe and handed it to the other, then clothed himself in his covenant brothers garments. "I am putting on you, and you

me. We are one". Picking up their weapons from the ground, each handed the other his sword, his bow. By this action they understood, "your enemies are now mine, and mine yours". Then they handed each other their belts, when you are weak, my strength will be there for you. In a figure eight path, both walked through the pieces of flesh lying opposite to each other, it was a walk into death. I am dying to my independent living and to my rights. They swore by an oath as they pointed first to heaven, "God do so to me" and then to the slain animals, "if I break this covenant". Then each made a cut and with their hands clasped the two men mingled their blood, "it is agreed once two, we have now become one". In turn each recited what they owned and what they owed. From this day forward they would share all their resources, "what's mine is yours, and what's yours is mine". Each reached down and scooped up dirt mixed with small stones and rubbed this abrasive into the cut in his wrist, "wherever I am when I lift my hand and see this scar, I will remember I have a covenant partner". They exchanged new names, "because of covenant I have a new identity". They sat down to partake of a covenant meal. One broke bread and placed it in his covenant partners mouth, and the other did the same, "you are consuming me, and I you". Finally a memorial was set up, a pile of stones, a planted tree, a written contract as a testimony of the covenant that they had made. "Now I call you friend, my friend who sticks closer than a brother".

The paragraph above is exactly what happened with Abraham in Genesis 15. Lets take a look at this passage:

"After these things the word of the Lord came to Abram in a vision, saying, "Do not fear, Abram, I am *a shield to you; Your reward shall be very great." ² Abram said, "O Lord God, what will You give me, since I am childless, and the heir of my house is Eliezer of Damascus?" ³ And Abram said, "Since You have given no offspring to me, one born in my house is my heir." ⁴ Then behold, the word of the Lord came to him, saying, "This man will not be your heir; but one who will come forth from your own body, he shall be your heir." ⁵ And He took him outside and said, "Now look toward the heavens, and count the stars, if you are able to count them." And He said to him, "So shall your descendants be." ⁶ Then he believed in the Lord; and He reckoned it to him as righteousness. ⁷ And He said to him, "I am the Lord who brought you out of Ur of the Chaldeans, to give you this land to possess it." ⁸ He said, "O Lord God, how may I know that I will possess it?" ⁹ So [God] said to him, "Bring Me a three year old heifer, and a three year old female goat, and a three year old ram, and a turtledove, and a young pigeon." ¹⁰ Then he brought all these to Him and cut them in two, and laid each half opposite the other; but he did not cut the birds. ¹¹ The birds of prey came down upon the carcasses, and Abram drove them away." - Genesis 15:1-11*

According to verse 10, what five animals did God tell Abraham to go get?

COVENANT IS AN EXCHANGE OF IDENTITIES

This is really amazing! God was cutting a covenant with Abraham! The two families were becoming one! Lets take a look symbolically at what they would exchange:

EXCHANGING ARMOR & WEAPONS: As the heads of the houses were standing in the blood, one of the things that they would exchange was armor and weapons. They would say, "Your enemies are now my enemies. Your friends are now my friends." This meant that if an enemy was coming for your covenant partner, you would hide them in your house and go out to fight on their behalf before you were willing for them to fight.

Look at what Paul says about God's armor and weapons in Ephesians 6:

[10] Finally, be strong in the Lord and in the strength of His might. [11] Put on the full armor of God, so that you will be able to stand firm against the schemes of the devil. [12] For our struggle is not against flesh and blood, but against the rulers, against the powers, against the world forces of this darkness, against the spiritual forces of wickedness in the heavenly places. [13] Therefore, take up the full armor of God, so that you will be able to resist in the evil day, and having done everything, to stand firm. [14] Stand firm therefore, having girded your loins with truth, and having put on the breastplate of righteousness, [15] and having shod your feet with the preparation of the gospel of peace; [16] in addition to all, taking up the shield of faith with which you will be able to extinguish all the flaming arrows of the evil one. [17] And take the helmet of salvation, and the sword of the Spirit, which is the word of God.

What does Ephesians 6:10-17 tell you to do?

EXCHANGING MANTLE, BELT & TOOLS: This meant that your abilities, gifts and talents were now in service to them and you both shared all resources, projects, tasks and burdens. This meant, you would help establish and build your partners house before you would build your own and you would supply their need before you would supply your own.

"33 But seek first His kingdom and His righteousness, and all these things will be added to you. 34 "So do not worry about tomorrow; for tomorrow will care for itself. Each day has enough trouble of its own." - Matthew 6:33-34

"And He called the twelve together, and gave them power and authority over all the demons and to heal diseases. 2 And He sent them out to proclaim the kingdom of God and to perform healing. 3 And He said to them, 'Take nothing for your journey, neither a staff, nor a bag, nor bread, nor money; and do not even have two tunics apiece. 4 Whatever house you enter, stay there until you leave that city. 5 And as for those who do not receive you, as you go out from that city, shake the dust off your feet as a testimony against them.' 6 Departing, they began going throughout the villages, preaching the gospel and healing everywhere." - Luke 9:1-6

What do the passages above tell you about trusting in Gods resources?

In Christ, God builds His kingdom out of the talents and resources we give to Him and we build our livelihood out of the grace He gives to us.

EXCHANGING NAMES: Especially in biblical times, names were like prophetic declarations that defined your destiny, identities and tribal alliances. Jesus often would give His followers new names on the spot. In Revelation it speaks of each one of us receiving a new name written on a white stone. We see God taking on the name of Abraham. *"I am the God of Abraham"* (Gen. 26:24) and we see God taking on the Name of the Gentiles (Rom 3:29).

"Peter said to them, 'Repent, and each of you be baptized in the name of Jesus Christ for the forgiveness of your sins; and you will receive the gift of the Holy Spirit." - Acts 2:38

According to the passage above, (see also Acts 8:16, 10:48, 19:5, 22:16, etc...) what name are we called to be baptized into?

EXCHANGING MEALS: A Meal was also exchanged in a covenant. In fact, in ancient culture, eating with someone was symbolic of complete acceptance into your family. It was also about sharing in the fruit of your harvest.

"⁴¹ So then, those who had received his word were baptized; and... ⁴² They were continually devoting themselves to the apostles' teaching and to fellowship, to the breaking of bread and to prayer... ⁴⁶ Day by day continuing with one mind in the temple, and breaking bread from house to house, they were taking their meals together with gladness and sincerity of heart, ⁴⁷ praising God and having favor with all the people. And the Lord was adding to their number day by day those who were being saved." - Acts 2:41-47

Is not the cup of blessing which we bless a sharing in the blood of Christ? Is not the bread which we break a sharing in the body of Christ? - 1 Corinthians 10:16

"[19] *For there must also be factions among you, so that those who are approved may become evident among you.* [20] *Therefore when you meet together, it is not to eat the Lord's Supper,* [21] *for in your eating each one takes his own supper first; and one is hungry and another is drunk.*" - 1 Corinthians 11:19-21

According to the passages above, what rite do believers practice regularly that involves a meal?

COVENANTS ARE INDIVIDUAL OR CORPORATE

Throughout the Bible, God may visit an individual and covenant with them in a specific way, or He could offer covenant to corporate group of people or a Nation. However, there are 8 major dispensational (time period) covenants that God makes with mankind in general and as a whole. These 8 dispensational covenants are recorded in the pages of the Bible. They explain God's relationship with man throughout history and the covenant to come in the future. We are currently in the seventh covenant and are about to enter into the eighth and final eternal covenant.

NOTE: More on these covenants can be found in Jacob's other book, "Covenant Relationship".

THREE ESSENTIAL INGREDIENTS TO EVERY TRUE COVENANT

There are three major components of every covenant. These three components are always established at the beginning of each covenant. These components are a testimony, a sacrifice, and a seal. In order for a covenant to be established and recognized by God as legitimate, it must begin with these three things.

1) A TESTIMONY: The testimony is a compilation of written vows or promises made to the potential spouse. It was called a testimony (or a testament) because it was the written testimony or promise that the one offering covenant was vowing their life to fulfill. Whenever God relates to man, He always first establishes a covenant. In His covenant, He clearly communicates what He is willing to offer, and what He expects in return.

2) A SACRIFICE: After the testimony is given, a sacrifice is made either symbolically or actually which communicates that the parties involved are forever sacrificing their independence and their independent way of living for the sake of becoming one in identity, ownership and aim with this other individual.

3) A SEAL: The "seal" is the final step in the process of establishing and consummating a covenant. A seal is the same as a "sign." It signifies that you are now in active covenant with someone else. Wedding rings act as seals of marriage covenant to many in our culture. Historically, sexual union between virgins is the seal and consummation of marital covenant. A seal is designed to give its

participants great faith and assurance and security in the relationship.

GOD IS A COVENANT KEEPER, THE DEVIL A DIVORCER

A Covenant is an unconditional self-sacrificing relationship. Not an agreement between two parties, but a union between two parties. There is no back door, no exit in a true covenant. You are forever committed regardless of what you get in return. It is a death-to-independence relationship. This might be scary for you if you are on the giving-end of the relationship, but consider the receiving-end. There is no fear on the receiving end. There is never a chance of abandonment or rejection in a covenant. In a true covenant, there is complete and absolute security.

"[God] Himself has said, 'I will never desert you, nor will I ever forsake you,'" -Hebrews 13:5

According to the passage above, what type of security does God offer in covenant with Him?

This is covenant language. He is always pursuing oneness with us, He is always waiting for us, always loving us. To enter any covenant, by definition one must forever cut off all independence of thought and intent for the sake of becoming one with another party. Satan hates covenant because it is the Promised Land for all believers. It is the bond between us and God, within Family, within the Church, within friendships, and within society! Satan knows this and he hates it. Divorce is not in the vocabulary of a true covenant because a covenant means sacrifice forever.

The word "Devil" is "Diabolos" in Greek. It comes from two root words in Greek, "Dia," which means, "through," and "Bolos," which means, "to cast." The term, "devil" literally means, "one who casts himself or something else in between two in order to separate them." In other words, the word "devil" means, "divider" or more accurately "divorcer." The devil is the anti-covenanter.

Stop for a moment and consider the ways the devil is trying to separate you from God, from family, from friends, from the Church. Do you see the devil's work for what it is now?

Many people suffer from deep wounds given intentionally or unintentionally by parents, friends, or the opposite sex who have failed to offer the security and identity found only within a covenant. Many of these are now severely handicapped when it comes to relationships and intimacy because of the unforgiveness, fear and insecurity that has resulted in their hearts.

Are there areas of un-forgiveness, fear, and insecurity that are affecting your current relationships that God wants to free you from?

ADOPTION IN ANCIENT HEBREW CULTURE

In the days of the Bible, if a family member did something to dishonor the family, the family could choose to disown the member. This meant the person was liable for their own actions and was no longer under the protection of the family. God didn't want anyone to disown anyone, but it was allowed in the case of unbearable or ridiculous dishonor. However, if a family was to adopt a child, the tradition stated you could never disown an adopted child. Again, adoption is a form of Covenant. It breaks the cycle of rejection and abandonment in a persons life. Covenant is even stronger than family.

"For you have not received a spirit of slavery leading to fear again, but you have received a spirit of adoption as sons by which we cry out, 'Abba! Father!'" - Romans 8:15

"...so that He might redeem those who were under the Law, that we might receive the adoption as sons." - Galatians 4:5

"He predestined us to adoption as sons through Jesus Christ to Himself, according to the kind intention of His will." - Ephesians 1:5

Understanding what "adoption" meant in biblical times, what do the passages above reveal about your position with God?

MARRIAGE IN ANCIENT HEBREW CULTURE

A marriage between a man and woman is meant to be a covenant relationship. During a wedding ceremony in our culture, there is generally a time to say your vows (the testimony), you are standing at an alter (to exemplify sacrifice) where you literally make a declaration to forever "cut" (or sacrifice) everything and anything of yourself that threatens the unity and wellbeing of this new relationship. Then you "seal the vows" with rings and sexual union (-both of which are seals) signifying that you are now in active covenant with each other. Although every relationship we have might not call for the commitment that a "forever" covenant relationship has, the principals of covenant can still be used to bless every relationship regardless of the level of commitment or calling of that relationship.

Hebrew marriage as a picture of the New Covenant with Christ

Much of what Jesus said and did were in direct context to covenant. In the Hebrew culture in the time of Jesus' incarnation, if a Jewish man wanted to enter into a marriage covenant with a woman, traditionally he would gather the three ingredients of covenant and as they were sharing a meal, he would muster up his courage and place those three things before the potential bride and her father. The three things included; A set of Promises or vows (the testimony), a Bride Price (the sacrifice), and a Cup of wine (the seal).

1) THE TESTIMONY (OR VOWS) -The testimony was usually a compilation of written vows or promises that the potential bridegroom swore or to fulfill to the bride and her family if they were to accept his proposal. Called a testimony (or a testament) because it was the written testimony or promise of truth that he would fulfill.

2) THE BRIDE PRICE - Second the potential groom would set a large sum of money or a receipt down. Every Jewish man traditionally would be saving up from an early age for his future bride. This money was passionately offered for two primary reasons. First it declared the Sacrifice he was willing to make for his bride, That she was the one that he has been saving up for since his birth. It was his sacrificial offering for her. The second thing that the bride price was given for was that it was also a way of paying back the family in thanksgiving for raising his bride and the soon-to-be the mother of his children.

3) THE CUP - A cup would be placed before her containing wine. If the potential bride and her father agreed to this covenant, the bride would take the cup and drink it signifying a "yes" or an "I do!" –This was her sign or the seal of her agreement and approval to the proposal.

Matthew 26:26-28 says, "While they were eating, Jesus took some bread, and after a blessing, He broke it and gave it to the disciples, and said, "Take, eat; this is My body." [27] *And when He had taken a cup and given thanks, He gave it to them, saying, "Drink from it, all of you;* [28] *for this is My blood of the covenant, which is poured out for many for forgiveness of sins."*

Understanding Covenant, what is Jesus saying in the passage above?

THE VEIL

It was also customary once the woman accepted the covenant in that day to wear a shawl or a veil wherever she went. She would draw it up and cover her face, saving her beauty only to be revealed to her groom upon entrance into the wedding chamber.

Matthew 27:51 says, "Suddenly the veil of the temple was torn in two from top to bottom, the earth shook, the rocks were split open." (See also Mark 15:38 and Luke 23:45)

The temple was called the dwelling place of God. The veil of the temple hid the presence of God from the outside world. What significance does this passage have for us who believe?

2 Corinthians 3:12-16 says, *"Therefore, since we have such a hope, we speak with great boldness, not like Moses, who kept covering his face with a veil to keep the people of Israel from gazing at the end of what was fading away. However, their minds were hardened. for to this day the same veil is still there when they read the old covenant. Only in union with Christ is that veil removed. Yet even to this day, when Moses is read, a veil covers their hearts. But whenever a person turns to the Lord, the veil is removed."*

What does this passage say about our veil?

ONLY THE FATHER KNOWS

After the proposal was accepted, the groom would return to his own father's house and begin building a wedding chamber that was either attached to his father's house or on his fathers property. At this point, the bride and her bridegroom were considered "engaged." The only thing they had to wait for was the "amen" of the father of the groom. Traditionally, the bridegroom built the wedding chamber, but it was his father that decided when it was complete. Often it would take over a year before the bridegroom had received his father's blessing and approval. The time that he spent building was another declaration to the bride of her worth to the bridegroom and his family.

In Matthew 24:1-28, Jesus gives about 15 descriptions of things that would transpire in the generation that sees His return. In verse 36 of this passage, it says, *"No one knows when that day or hour will come-not the angels in heaven, nor the Son, but only the Father."* What is this passage saying about the exact day of His return?

John 14:1-3 says, "Do not let your hearts be troubled. Believe in God, believe also in me. There are many rooms in my Father's house. If there were not, would I have told you that I am going away to prepare a place for you? And if I am going away to prepare a place for you, I will come again and will welcome you into my presence, so you may be where I am."

What does this passage say about what Christ is currently doing?

THE BRIDESMAIDS

It was also often tradition for the father of the groom to give his "amen" during the night after dinner. At that point the bridegroom would rush over to the bride's house and call to her.

Matthew 25:1-13 says, "At that time, the kingdom of heaven will be compared to ten bridesmaids who took their oil lamps and went out to meet the groom. Now five of them were foolish, and five were wise. For when the foolish ones took their lamps, they didn't take any oil with them. But the wise ones took flasks of oil with their lamps. Since the groom was late, all of them became sleepy and lay down. "But at midnight there came a shout: 'The groom is here! Come out to meet him!' Then all the bridesmaids woke up and got their lamps ready. But the foolish ones said to the wise, 'Give us some of your oil, for our lamps are going out!' But the wise ones replied, 'No! There will never be enough for us and for you. Better go to the dealers and buy some for yourselves.' "While they were away buying it, the groom arrived. Those who were ready went with him into the wedding banquet, and the door was closed. Later the other bridesmaids arrived and said, 'Lord, lord, open up for us!' But he replied, 'Truly I tell you, I don't know you!' So keep on watching, because you don't know the day or the hour."

Name a few things that this passage teaches between the similarities of the Hebrew wedding and the second coming of Christ for His church.

THE WEDDING SUPPER

As she came out with her bridesmaids, they would all be escorted to the grooms house where they would feast and the couple would enter wedding chamber and spend a week there without coming out. Meanwhile, the fathers would throw a huge wedding party. while the families and friends partied.

Matthew 22:1-14 says, "Again Jesus spoke to them in parables. He said, 'The kingdom of heaven may be compared to a king who gave a wedding banquet for his son. He sent his servants to call those who had been invited to the wedding, but they refused to come. So he sent other servants, saying, 'Tell those who have been invited, "Look, I've prepared my dinner. My oxen and fattened calves have been slaughtered. Everything is ready. Come to the wedding!"' But they paid no attention to this and went away, one to his farm, another to his business. The rest grabbed the king's servants, treated them brutally, and then killed them. Then the king became outraged. He sent his troops, and they destroyed those murderers and burned their city. 'Then he said to his servants, 'The wedding is ready, but those who were invited were not worthy. So go into the roads leading out of town and invite as many people as you can find to the wedding.' Those servants went out into the streets and brought in all the people they found, evil and good alike, and the wedding hall was packed with guests. "When the king came in to see the guests, he noticed a man there who was not wearing wedding clothes. He said to him, 'Friend, how did you get in here without wedding clothes?' But the man was speechless. Then the king told his servants, 'Tie his hands and feet, and throw him into the outer darkness! In that place there will be weeping and gnashing of teeth.' For many are invited, but few are chosen."*

What does the passage above say about those who are invited to the wedding?

Revelation 19:9 says, "Then the angel said to me, "Write this: 'How blessed are those who are invited to the marriage supper of the lamb!'"

What does the passage above tell you about those who are called to the wedding supper of the Lamb?

THE TESTIMONY OF THE NEW COVENANT

As we saw in Book one of this series, the Scriptures are to be viewed as "the Word of God." However, in many church cultures, there seems to be a lack of understanding as to the purpose of the scriptures. It seams by lack of understanding "testimony," many people hold the scriptures in an unproductive, or even harmful way.

A CORRECT VIEW OF SCRIPTURE

Throughout the Bible, the word "testimony" is used many times. It literally means "evidence" or "witness". In the Old Testament it referred to the two tablets that God gave to Moses upon which God had written the Ten Commandments. This was to be a "testimony" (witness) for or against them in years to come. When we say the Old "Testament" we are referring to the accepted "testimony" of the old covenant. Likewise, when we say the New "Testament" we are referring to the accepted "testimony" of the New Covenant which likewise is a witness which testifies to "what we should expect out of a relationship with God in this age."

Here we will look at two types of people who's wrong view of scripture caused them to miss

Jesus Himself. During the time of the incarnation, two of the most prevalent religious sects within judaism were called the Sadducees and the Pharisees. They represented what we might consider the liberal and conservative branches of politics and religion.

THE PHARISEES

The Pharisees could be considered as the "religious conservatives" of Jesus' day. In history, they were the ones who didn't compromise their traditions when the Greeks and Romans historically put pressure on the Jewish people. They prided themselves on keeping to the traditions, knowing the scriptures and being spiritually "correct." They erred on being superficial, hypocritical, prideful and having unmerciful judgment. They interpreted the scriptures literally, but in general, many of them failed to know the heart of God.

"Do not judge so that you will not be judged. ² For in the way you judge, you will be judged; and by your standard of measure, it will be measured to you. ³ Why do you look at the speck that is in your brother's eye, but do not notice the log that is in your own eye? ⁴ Or how can you say to your brother, 'Let me take the speck out of your eye,' and behold, the log is in your own eye? ⁵ You hypocrite, first take the log out of your own eye, and then you will see clearly to take the speck out of your brother's eye." -Matthew 7:1-5

You search the Scriptures because you think that in them you have eternal life; it is these that testify about Me; - John 5:39

What do the previous passages tell you about Jesus' views toward religious judgment and the purpose of the Scriptures?

THE SADDUCEES

The Sadducees or "Hellenistic Jews" could be considered the "religious liberals" of Jesus' day. In history, they were the sect of Jewish people who forsook the traditions to embrace the greco-roman culture. When Greece, and then Rome took over and tempted the Jews with positions of leadership over the people, the Sadducees were the ones who took the jobs. Sadducees were Jewish priests appointed not by the Jews, but by the Roman government to act as religious leaders over the people. They were looked at by many as sell-outs who compromised the traditions for the sake of rank or greed. The Sadducees didn't take the Scriptures literally. They had accepted Greek philosophical thought which questions the supernatural or "unseen" realm.

"But perceiving that one group were Sadducees and the other Pharisees, Paul began crying out in the Council, "Brethren, I am a Pharisee, a son of Pharisees; I am on trial for the hope and resurrection of the dead!" ⁷ As he said this, there occurred a dissension between the Pharisees and Sadducees, and the assembly was divided. ⁸ For the Sadducees say that there is no resurrection, nor an angel, nor a spirit, but the Pharisees acknowledge them all. ⁹ And there occurred a great uproar; and some of the scribes of the Pharisaic party stood up and began to argue heatedly, saying, "We find nothing wrong with this man; suppose a spirit or an angel has

spoken to him?" ¹⁰ And as a great dissension was developing, the commander was afraid Paul would be torn to pieces by them and ordered the troops to go down and take him away from them by force, and bring him into the barracks." - Acts 23:6-10

What does Acts 23:6-10 tell you about the Sadducees?

"²³ On that day some Sadducees (who say there is no resurrection) came to Jesus and questioned Him, ²⁴ asking, "Teacher, Moses said, 'If a man dies having no children, his brother as next of kin shall marry his wife, and raise up children for his brother.' ²⁵ Now there were seven brothers with us; and the first married and died, and having no children left his wife to his brother; ²⁶ so also the second, and the third, down to the seventh. ²⁷ Last of all, the woman died. ²⁸ In the resurrection, therefore, whose wife of the seven will she be? For they all had married her." ²⁹ But Jesus answered and said to them, "You are mistaken, not understanding the Scriptures nor the power of God. ³⁰ For in the resurrection they neither marry nor are given in marriage, but are like angels in heaven. ³¹ But regarding the resurrection of the dead, have you not read what was spoken to you by God: ³² 'I am the God of Abraham, and the God of Isaac, and the God of Jacob'? He is not the God of the dead but of the living." ³³ When the crowds heard this, they were astonished at His teaching." - Matthew 22:23-33

According to verse 23 in the passage above, what self-imposed disadvantage did the Sadducees have that made it difficult for any of them to believe in Jesus? What is Jesus' initial response in verse 29?

As you can see from the Scriptures above, both the Pharisees and the Sadducees had the wrong view of the Scriptures. Both parties missed Jesus. The Pharisees persecuted Him and the Sadducees had no context for Him.

The Pharisees used the Scriptures to find fault with those who did not fit into their "brand." They prided themselves on Bible reading, praying, giving; -things that most conservative Christians do today, but they ended up becoming enemies against the biggest move of God in history.

The Sadducees didn't take the Scriptures literally. They prided themselves on being tolerant and embracing other ideas and cultures like most liberal Christians do today. Yet because of their over-appreciation for cultural awareness and their under-appreciation for their biblical traditions, they failed to recognize their own Messiah.

Please take some time to pray for yourself, your friends, your family and your church knowing that these things are likely to apply to you.

TESTIMONIES, VOWS AND PROMISES

Every time the word "promise" is used in the Bible, it is in context to covenant. As it was said earlier, throughout Old Testament History, whenever God desires to establish a Covenant relationship with a generation of people, the first thing He does is He establishes and clearly communicates all of the set promises (the testimony of abundance, deliverance, and consequences) that He binds Himself to within that certain covenant. He is very intentional and purposeful with these promises. Each covenant has a promise and the promise of God to us in the New Covenant is written down and found as the whole of the New Testament. The New Testament is His love letter to us—His vows—the witness of His loving intention toward us who believe. The New Testament is the testimony of the New Covenant!

While God's New Covenant love and favor are unconditional, the specific promises within the New Covenant generally are conditional. Most of the individual promises of God in the New Testament will generally have a few set conditions attached to them. After understanding the idea behind a "Vassal" Covenant, it is easy to understand that if we (or our culture) are not willing to submit ourselves to the conditions of His covenant; we are not entitled to become recipients of the blessings of His covenant.

In the New Covenant, God's promises are many. The following verses are a few among hundreds of New Covenant promises. After reading the scriptures below, please highlight the specific promises <u>and</u> conditions given in each.

Matthew 7:9-11, [9] Or what man is there among you who, when his son asks for a loaf, will give him a stone? [10] Or if he asks for a fish, he will not give him a snake, will he? [11] If you then, being evil, know how to give good gifts to your children, how much more will your Father who is in heaven give what is good to those who ask Him!

Mark 16:17-18, These signs will accompany those who have believed: in My name they will cast out demons, they will speak with new tongues; 18 they will pick up serpents, and if they drink any deadly poison, it will not hurt them; they will lay hands on the sick, and they will recover."

John 3:16, "For God so loved the world, that He gave His only begotten Son, that whoever believes in Him shall not perish, but have eternal life.

Acts 3:19, "Therefore repent and return, so that your sins may be wiped away, in order that times of refreshing may come from the presence of the Lord;

Romans 8:28 - "And we know that God causes all things to work together for good to those who love God, to those who are called according to His purpose."

It is important that Christians believe that every one of the promises found in the pages of the New Testament are free gifts of grace which are applicable for every person (Jew or Gentile, slave or free, male or female -Gal 3:28) who is willing to receive and abide by them. The Glorious promises of Christ are not just for the apostles, but *"for those also who believe in Me (Jesus) through their word"* - John 17:20!

4

HE SPEAKS THROUGH THE HEBREW LANGUAGE

THE HEBREW LANGUAGE

As we have clarified in previous chapters, God's ability to communicate predates and transcends all of man's languages and vocabularies. We have learned how Christ, the Man, was the ultimate form of communication from God. The Word became flesh because human vocabulary alone can never fully express the fullness of who God is. So Jesus came and His life continues to speak universally through every culture, language and generation.

While Jesus Christ is the ultimate, universal Word of God to us, God also uses a number of other "universal languages" to speak to us. One of these universal languages is delivered in the form of pictures. A picture is a universal language that can communicate the same thing to someone who speaks Mandarin in China as it does to someone who speaks Spanish in Venezuela. When we survey the Scriptures, we find God using natural means as well as spiritual means to paint pictures that communicate to us.

We bring this up because the Hebrew language is a pictorial language. It is truly beautiful. Each letter in the Aleph-bet usually has at least three meanings: a letter, a number and a picture. For instance, the letter "bet" which is equivalent to the English letter "B" also carries the numeric value of "2" and it's pictorial meaning is "house" or "dwelling place." This triple meaning of every letter makes the Hebrew language one of the more poetically and prophetically abundant languages known to man. Think about it, every word is made of a series of numbers and/or letters, each letter with its own word meaning and numeric value! The deeper meanings of everything is infinite!

THE POLARITIES OF INTERPRETATION

Please note that pictorial language is more subjective than verbal language. Pictures require interpretation even more than words do. "What does that mean?" This is often the question we ask when we receive a picture from God. While each Hebrew letter (or pictograph) carries a meaning, that meaning might be interpreted differently depending on the views of the one interpreting it. How you interpret something often tells you more about the condition of your heart than it does the thing you are interpreting.

For instance, the letter ז, which is "Zayin" in Hebrew. This letter is the equivalent to the English "Z" and has the numeric value of 7. Its pictograph and word meaning is "sword." Say two prophets had the same vision and saw this number hovering over Jerusalem. They both came together and one said, "I saw a sword hovering over Jerusalem. War is coming!" The other one said, "I saw the same thing, but I do not believe God was speaking of a sword, but the number seven. God is going to bring Sabbath rest to Jerusalem. There will not be war." See the difference? The way you see and interpret determines almost everything.

In the space provided under the following passages, please note what the passage teaches on the art of interpretation.

"It is the glory of God to conceal a matter, But the glory of kings is to search out a matter." - Proverbs 25:2

"...Nothing is hidden that will not become evident, nor anything secret that will not be known and come to light. So take care how you listen." - Luke 8:17-18

"The good man out of the good treasure of his heart brings forth what is good; and the evil man out of the evil treasure brings forth what is evil; for his mouth speaks from that which fills his heart." - Luke 6:45

Maybe God chose the Hebrew language to be the first one that His Torah was known through because He is more interested in revealing hearts than facts. Leaving things up to interpretation forces us to have an opinion and in that opinion we discover a lot about who we are. For instance, many people believe the coming of God's kingdom means a future judgment and wrath for sinners. To others the coming of God's kingdom means forgiveness, salvation and healing for sinners. These are two polar opposite opinions. The question some might pose is, "What if we stopped warning of the signs of the coming of Christ and His kingdom and began being the signs of the coming of Christ and His Kingdom?"

In God's Kingdom there is room for interpretation. Both ends of even this spectrum are included in Christ. Some might become agitated by this paradox, but it is important to not become so rigid in these things. *"A bended reed He shall not break." - Matthew 12:20*

THE HEBREW ALEPH-BET

We have offered the Hebrew Aleph-Bet below with each letter's numeric value and pictorial meaning. For anyone who operates prophetically in any way, knowing the Hebrew aleph-bet will prove a tremendous resource for helping you to accurately interpret your prophetic dreams and visions for years to come.

Please use a concordance or bible software to look up the word most associated with each Hebrew pictograph. For instance, "Aleph" is a pictograph of an "Ox." Look up "Ox" or "Bull" in a concordance and you will find many scriptures that speak of the Ox. After viewing these scriptures, please use the space provided under each letter to write out the passage that carries the greatest revelatory value.

א - ALEPH (silent) (1 or 1000) / Meanings: OX, ONENESS, LEADER, LORD

The aleph is the father of the Aleph-Bet. The pictograph of the Aleph represents an ox. Traditionally it has been taken to mean strength, or leader. As the number one, it means union, singleness, or oneness. Its closest related word is "Aluph" which means "Master" or "Lord." The three sections of the Aleph can also be taken to represent the three realms; the divine realm of heaven (top yod), the human realm of earth (bottom yod) and the dual natured realm that joins the two (the person of Christ).

* "Hear, O Israel: The Lord our God, the Lord is one." - Deuteronomy 6:4 (ESV)

‏ב - BET (b,v) (2) / Meanings: HOUSE

The pictograph and word meaning of the Bet is "House" or "Dwelling place." This letter represents our home in Christ and His home in us. There are many scriptures in the Bible regarding the "House of God." Every placement of "bet" is a reminder of those truths. As the number two, it also represents duality, or the joining together in partnership, companionship, witness and/or support. Historically, many sages and rabbi's taught that "bet" represents the divine balance in creation, as the Genesis account records almost everything as being created in twos; day and night, land and sea, plants and trees, sun and moon, male and female, etc...
* "Two cherubim guarded the Ark of the Covenant" (Exodus 25:22)
* Two witnesses establish truth (Matthew 26:60),
* The disciples were sent two by two (Luke 10:1)

‏ג - GIMEL (g) (3) / Meanings: REWARD OR REBUKE

The pictograph of the Gimel is a Camel which in ancient culture was an animal of great provision, help and strength. The word *gimel* is derived from the word gemul, which in Hebrew means both the giving of reward as well as the giving of punishment. In some jewish writings the Gimel is described as a rich man running after a poor man to bring charity. As the letter three, Gimel represents stability and strength as well as perfection. There are many significant events in the Bible happened "on the third day" (Hosea 6:2), or in three years (Luke 13:7). In Hebrew culture, the fruit

of a tree was not to be considered mature until the tree was at least three years old, and the fruit of a man (his teaching) was not to be considered mature until he was at least thirty years old.
* "A cord of three *strands* is not quickly torn apart. "(Ecclesiastes 4:12)
* Jonah spent three days and three nights in the belly of the fish (Matthew 12:40).
* Jesus' earthly ministry lasted three years (Luke 13:7).
* "Jesus answered them, 'Destroy this temple, and in three days I will raise it up.'" (John 2:19 - ESV)

ד - DALET (d) (4) / Meanings: DOOR, EARTHS CREATED ORDER, POVERTY

The Dalet symbolizes a bent over, needy person or servant. The root word "Dalut" means impoverished or poor. This letter symbolizes lowliness or humility. The pictograph of the Dalet can also be seen as a "door." As a door, the Dalet represents the threshold between two places. It can symbolize the entrance into a new dwelling or lifestyle, and/or the exit of an old dwelling or lifestyle. In other words it represents the opening and/or closing of a season. Historically, many have found significance in the Dalet as a representation of God's divine government and order; earth has four seasons: winter, spring, summer, fall. Earth also has four primary directions: north, south, east, west.
* Bible describes four earthly kingdoms (Daniel 7:3)
* Four living creatures (Rev. 4:6)
* Four human conditions of the heart (Matthew 13).

* Four corners of the earth - Isaiah 11:12 - "He will raise a signal for the nations and will assemble the banished of Israel, and gather the dispersed of Judah from the four corners of the earth." (ESV)

ה - HEY (h) (5) / Meanings: CREATIVE UTTERANCE OR PRAISE

The Hey is a pictograph of a man with arms raised. This word is used as an exclamation to "Look" or "Behold." Together, it is a man, with arms raised to heaven, proclaiming "Look!" As it is also the natural sound of an exhaling person and it is impossible to say, "hey" without exhaling, it symbolizes Divine Breath or Creative Utterance. Psalm 33:6 says "by the ['Hey'] of His mouth the heavens were made..." It is uniquely special in that it is the only letter used twice in the name of God, YHWH. As the number five, "Hey" also has great biblical significance.
* There are five [hey] Levitical offerings (Leviticus 1-5).
* Jesus multiplied five loaves of barely to feed 5,000 (Matthew 14:17).

ו - WAW or VAV (v,w) (6) / Meanings: HOLDING, SECURING OR CONSECRATING

The Pictograph of a Vav is a tent peg, sword or hook. It represents the holding, establishing or securing of a person, place or thing. It represents the thing that both cuts away and binds to. It is the both the means of consecration as well as the means of union. It is the binding agent making two into one. The tent peg was used to assemble the tabernacle. As six, it is the number of man and represents man, as man was created on the sixth day. It pictures man (in Christ) as the connection between heaven and earth. It is the tent peg who's movement determines the parameters of the boundary of God's earthly tabernacle. It represents God establishing His covenantal tent on earth through the incarnate body of the man, Jesus Christ, and man being hooked and woven into the tabernacle of heaven through the same incarnation of Christ's body.

* Adam and Eve were created on the sixth day (Genesis 1:31).
* Numbers 35:6 - "The cities that you give to the Levites shall be the six cities of refuge, where you shall permit the manslayer to flee ..." (ESV)

ז - ZAYIN (z) (7) / Meanings: VICTORY, COMPLETION, REST

The Pictograph of a Zayin is a sword or a vav with crown on its head. The crown on top of the sword means there has been victory and now the sword can be put to rest, or at least put to a different task. This represents victory of the sword, victory in battle, or completed work. As God rested on the seventh day after completing the six days of creation, this letter represents a completed work, or job well done, the ending of the war, the consecration of the land. Seven is how God measures time. It represents a complete cycle. Christ is the Sword of the Spirit, the utterance of God, and He is victorious in battle. Seven is considered the number of God, meaning divine perfection or completeness.

* On the seventh day God rested after completing the creation (Genesis 2:2).

* God's Word is pure, like silver purified seven times in the fire (Psalm 12:6).
* Jesus taught Peter to forgive 70 times seven (Matthew 18:22).
* Seven demons went out from Mary Magdalene, symbolizing total deliverance (Luke 8:2).
* Exodus 21:2 - "When you buy a Hebrew slave, he shall serve six years, and in the seventh he shall go out free, for nothing." (ESV)

ח - HET or CHET (h,(ch)) (8) / Meanings: NEW BEGINNINGS, HOLINESS

The letter Het is made up of two letters, the Vav and the Zayin. The pictograph of Het is a wall or fence. This letter is viewed as very positive. In Hebrew, the words for "wisdom," "righteousness," "grace," and "life" all start with the letter Het. The numerical value of the letter Het is eight, which is often associated with super-spirituality or holiness, as it is one more than seven, which represents the holy realm of the Sabbath. When Jewish boys are circumcised and enter into their faith's holy ancient covenant, it is commanded to be performed on the eighth day (Genesis 17:12), marking the beginning of of his life. It represents new beginnings for a number of reasons;
* In the creation account, the eighth day comes after the "week" of creation (Gen. 1-2)
* Eight people survived the flood (Genesis 7:13, 23) and were saved to establish a new beginning for mankind,
* Sukkot is an 8 day festival that anticipate the *Olam Habah* - the world to come.

* Jesus was resurrected on the 1st day of the week, which if we understand the preceding seven days to constitute a complete cycle, is the eighth day.
* John 20:26 - "Eight days later, his disciples were inside again, and Thomas was with them. Although the doors were locked, Jesus came and stood among them and said, "Peace be with you." (ESV)

ט - TET (t) (9) / Meanings: VEILED SURPRISE, MANIFESTATION OF GOOD OR EVIL

The Pictograph of a Tet is a paradox in that it means veiled good or evil. Tet represents a decision between good and evil. The form of the letter is "inverted," suggesting hidden goodness, like that of a woman who is pregnant with child. However, sometimes the potential for goodness is perverted, and impurity or filth (a serpent) results. As a dichotomy, it represents the two possibilities of man, bowing to a serpent or bowing to a King. As the number nine, it symbolizes the following fullness of Spiritual blessing:
* There are nine gifts of the Spirit (1 Corinthians 12:8-11)
* There are also nine fruits of the Spirit (Galatians 5:22-23).

י - YOD (y) (10) / Meanings: GOD'S OMNIPRESENCE, LAW & ORDER

The pictograph for Yod is an arm or hand. Yod is the most frequently occurring letter in the Scriptures as well as the smallest of the letters. As the smallest

letter it is considered the "atom" of the consonants, and the source from which all of the other letters begin and end. Since Jesus upholds the world by the Word of His power (Hebrews 1:3), and Yod is part of every Hebrew letter and word, Yod is considered the symbol of the presence of Christ in all things. It represents the "spark" of the anointing present in everything at every time and also in concentrated points of specific time and space. As Yod represents a hand, and it is the number ten, we discover this letter symbolizes the giving of a "tithe" (literally a "10th") of our earnings. As the number ten, the Yod represents complete law and order for a number of reasons:
* In Genesis 1 we find the phrase "God said" ten times.
* God created the universe with ten utterances.
* The Ten Commandments were given as the foundation of the Law of Israel (Exodus 20:1-17, Deuteronomy 5:6-21).
* Ruth 4:2 - "And he [Boaz] took ten men of the elders of the city [as judges]..." (ESV)

כ - KAF (k,kh) (20) / Meanings: TO OBTAIN OR MANIFEST, WAITING

The pictograph of a Kaf is the palm of a hand. It symbolizes the obtaining or manifestation of something. In Jewish Mysticism, the two letters of the word "kaf" are the initial letters of the two Hebrew words: *koach* ("potential") and *poel* ("actual"), suggesting that Kaf enables the latent power of the spiritual (the potential) to be made actual in the physical. The literal meaning of Kaf is "palm" which is considered the location where potential of the Yod (hand) is actualized. For this reason we lay the

palms of our hands on the sick as we envision God having His palms over us. As the number twenty, Kaf can symbolize a complete or perfect waiting period for the following reasons;
- * For 20 years Jacob waited to get possession of his wives and property, and to be freed from the control of Laban his father-in-law (Genesis 31:38 - 41)
- * For 20 years the children of Israel waited to be freed of Jabin, king of Canaan, who oppressed them until God freed them trough Deborah and Barak (Judges 4 - 5).
- * Israel had to wait at least 20 years before they could move the Ark of the covenant out of Kirjath-jearim (1Samuel 5 - 7).
- * It took Solomon 20 years to build both his home in Jerusalem along with the temple of God (1Kings 9:10 - 11).

ל - LAMED (l) (30) / Meanings: STAFF, GOAD, DISCIPLESHIP

The Lamed is a pictograph of a Shepherds Staff or Goad. The Hebrew name of the letter itself, *lamed*, comes from the root *lamad* meaning to learn or teach or practice authority. It represents discipline or discipleship as a shepherd uses his staff to guide his sheep, so too a teacher disciplines his students. As the Lamed is the middle letter in the aleph-bet and it is also by far the tallest letter, it represents the King of Kings, enthroned and surrounded by the host of heaven. As the number thirty, it can represent human value or worth for a number of reasons:
- * Aaron's death was mourned for 30 days (Numbers 20:29).

* Moses' death was also mourned for 30 days (Deuteronomy 34:8).
* In Hebrew culture, it was customary that the teachings or fruit of a priest and rabbi not be received until they were 30 years of age.
* Jesus was betrayed for 30 pieces of silver (Matthew 27:3-5). - "Then when Judas, his betrayer, saw that Jesus was condemned, he changed his mind and brought back the thirty pieces of silver to the chief priests and the elders, saying, "I have sinned by betraying innocent blood." They said, "What is that to us? See to it yourself." And throwing down the pieces of silver into the temple, he departed, and he went and hanged himself." (ESV)

מ - MEM (m) (40) / Meanings: WOMB, WATERS, NATIONS, PEOPLES

The Mem is made up of two letters, the Kaf and the Vav. The pictograph of Mem is a womb or wave of water. As a womb and as water, it symbolizes peoples, Nations, languages and tongues. Just like in birth, as the water breaks to release what is in the womb, in the days of Noah, the flood came to release a new birth. Historically, anything that was under the surface of the water or the land was considered in the grave, or Sheol ("hell" in many English translations). The surface of the water represents the plane between life and death. This is why water baptism is practiced as the symbol of our union into the death, burial and resurrection of Christ. Waves and water also speak of danger, vastness and mystery. As the number 40, Mem is a number associated with testing and trials with a number of biblical examples:

* During the flood it rained 40 days (Genesis 7:4),
* Israel wandered in the desert for 40 years (Numbers 14:33).
* Jesus was in the wilderness 40 days before being <u>tempted</u> (Matthew 4:2).
* Exodus 24:18 - "Moses entered the cloud and went up on the mountain [Sinai]. And Moses was on the mountain forty days and forty nights." <u>(ESV)</u>

ן - NUN (n) (50) / Meanings: FISH, HUMBLED MAN, FAITHFUL

According to the Hebrew sages, Nun is said to represent both faithfulness and the reward for faithfulness. The word "Nun" itself is spelled Nun-Vav-Zayin, meaning, faithful one (bent one) and righteous one (upright one), meaning one who went from a faithful servant to a righteous heir (see James 4:10). The pictograph of Nun is a seed. Represents faithfulness and the reward for faithfulness. The word "Nun" is "fish" in Aramaic, which is a symbol of mans lower activity and life. The symbol of the fish has early roots in Christianity as an emblem of Jesus Christ. The word for fish in Greek is "ixthus," which some believe was used as an acronym for the Greek phrase *Yesous Christos Theou Uios Soter,* or "Jesus Christ the Son of God Savior." The first mention of the word is in Exodus 33:11, in reference to Joshua, the "son of Nun." Joshua, the one who succeeded Moses and was able to enter the Promised Land, was the "Son of man," - a clear picture of Jesus our Messiah. The original form of the Nun shows a bent Vav (suggesting a humbled man) crowned with glory (with three tagin on the head of the letter). From the Messianic point of view, we see that Jesus came as a man (Vav), was honored by His absolute humility while upon earth (as indicated by the crown of thorns), and is now exalted as the Righteous One who wears the Golden Crown of God upon His head forever and ever (Rev 14:14). As the number 50, Nun also has great significance, especially in feasts, celebrations, and ceremonies:

* The Feast of Pentecost was celebrated on the fiftieth day after Passover (Leviticus 23:15-16)
* 50 days after Jesus Christ's resurrection the Holy Spirit filled believers on the Day of Pentecost (Acts 2).
* In the Hebrew calendar, the 50th year is the jubilee of jubilees, or the year following the seventh cycle of seven weeks of years (7x7years =49years).
* Leviticus 25:10 - "And you shall consecrate the fiftieth year, and proclaim liberty throughout the land to all its inhabitants. It shall be a jubilee for you, when each of you shall return to his property and each of you shall return to his clan." (ESV)

ס - SAMECH (s) (60) / Meanings: TO IMPART (LAY ON HANDS, TO SHEILD

The pictograph of Samech has been referred to in two major ways, some have said it represents a shield and others have said it represents the "circle of life" or a "full cycle." As a circle, it represents the endless cycle of universe going from Glory to glory throughout every generation. The root of the word for *Samech* is found in the Jewish concept of *semikhah*, which is the "laying on of hands," which was the practice used by the Hebrews before God to indicated the transferral of authority, power, guilt and/or judgment (Lev 8; Exodus 29, Lev. 8, 16:21, Deut 34:9, Ezekiel 24:2, 29, etc...). This is what many patriarchs would do as they grew old, they would call the next generation and lay their hands on them and impart or delegate blessing, power and responsibility. The root word literally means "to lean upon," "to uphold," or "to support." The letter Samech represents the number 60, and some of the Jewish sages have noted that this is the same number of letters found in the *Birkat Kohanim* - the "Priestly Blessing" found in Numbers 6:23-27.

* Exodus 29:10 - "Then you shall bring the bull before the tent of meeting. Aaron and his sons *shall lay (samakh)* their hands on the head of the bull."

ע - AYIN (silent) (70) / Meanings: TO SEE, UNDERSTAND, LIGHT

The word *Ayin* means "eye," "to see," and by extension, to understand and obey (see Jer. 5:21, Isa. 6:10, Matt. 13:15, etc.). It represents revelation, understanding and ability. Ayin further represents the divine light or revelation from God (in contrast to natural or celestial lights mentioned in Gen. 1:14-18), which can only fully be perceived by those who have been born in the Spirit. As the number 70, Ayin has a possible association with human delegations and/or judgment for the following reasons:

* There were 70 elders were appointed by Moses (Numbers 11:16)
* There were 70 descendants of Jacob who went down into Egypt and later emerged with multitudes (Deuteronomy 10:22)
* Israel spent 70 years in captivity in Babylon (Jeremiah 29:10).

* Ezekiel 8:11- "And before them stood seventy men of the elders of the house of Israel, with Jaazaniah the son of Shaphan standing among them. Each had his censer in his hand, and the smoke of the cloud of incense went up." (ESV)

פ - PEY / PHEY (p,ph) (80) / Meanings: MOUTH, WORD, EXPRESSION, VOCALIZATION

The word *Peh* means "mouth" and by extension, "word," "expression," "vocalization," "speech," and "breath." In the order of the Hebrew alphabet, Pey follows the letter 'Ayin, suggesting the priority of the eyes (i.e., understanding, awareness) before verbal expression (negatively, reversing this order results in "blind consumption" or mindless chatter). The *chokhmah* (wise one) is swift to observe and *then* to offer an opinion about something. 'Ayin gives insight, but it is the *peh* (mouth) that gives expression to the insight. Since *peh* (mouth) follows 'ayin (eye), certain Jewish mystics have said that the Ayin is the gateway to truth, but the mouth is what brings truth into being. Many kabbalists claim that the letter Pey is composed of two other letters: Kaf and Yod. Since one of the meanings of Kaf is "container" (i.e., spoon), it is suggested that the letter Pey is a picture of the divine spark (Yod) of God within the soul (Kaf, understood as a container for the soul). The letter Pey represents the number 80. The number 80 also the age of Moses when he was called to lead the Children of Israel out of Egypt, and seems to be indicative of a sign of strength in human life.
  * Psalm 90:10 - "As for the days of our life, they contain seventy years, Or if due to strength,

eighty years, Yet their pride is but labor and sorrow; For soon it is gone and we fly away."

צ - Tzadi (ts) (90) / Meanings: RIGHTEOUSNESS, TO HUNT OR CAPTURE

The pictograph for Tzadi looks something like a man, laying on his side and reaching up (which can represent need or praise). *Tzadi* got its name from the shape of a "fishing hook" or perhaps a bird trap, which is related to the root *tzod*, meaning "to hunt, catch, capture." Notice that the letter itself is formed from a bent Nun and a Vav. The Nun represents a humble and faithful servant (the crowned Vav) that is bent in submission. The Yod represents a hand lifted to heaven, or the Spirit of God.

Tzadi is the root of *tzaddik*, which means "righteous person" and is therefore revealed in the letter form as a faithful servant with his arms raised before the LORD in humility. As such, some of the sages have said that the letter Tzadi represents the *tzaddikim* (righteous ones) that are the *yesod* (foundation) of the earth: "When the storm passes through, the wicked are swept away, but the righteous are an everlasting foundation." (Prov 10:25) Since God alone is perfectly righteous and upright *(tzaddik v'yashar* - Deut 32:4), and His righteousness is the only true foundation of the universe, the *tzaddik* is said to reflect the divine image within us *(b'tzelem elohim)* when we live in humility and dependence upon Him for the ability to live in trusting obedience to His will. "Behold, his soul is puffed up; it is not upright within him, but the righteous shall live by his faith." (Hab 2:4) Other words that suggest a

connection between obedience and righteousness are *tzedek* (righteous) and *tzedakah* (righteous deeds, righteousness). Just as the *melakhim* (angels) are God's messengers in heaven, so the *tzaddikim* are said to be God's messengers upon the earth.
* The numerical value of Tzadi is 90 which is significant in Jewish tradition as the fulness of life, cs Pirkei Avot 5:21

ק - QOF (q) (100) / Meanings: SUN ON HORIZON, THE PAST OR FUTURE, STITCHED TOGETHER

In its ancient form, the Qof was turned on its side, representing a sun on a horizon. Its original meaning was therefore symbolized time, and especially the past (or beginning) or the future (or end) depending on if it was sunset or sunrise. Later, the Qof became pictured vertical and commonly became associated with "An eye of a needle" as this is the literal meaning of Qof in Aramaic. As a needle, its meaning has centered on its ability to attach two things together, making them one.
* Qof words include Kadosh (holy). The holiness of God is His "specialness". He is to be honored above all else.
* Korban (sacrifice) is also a Qof word.
* Qof comes from the root Karev which means to come close.
* A Qof year (age 100) is a year to come closer to God or to go home to meet God.

ר - RESH (r) (200) / Meanings: HEAD, LEADER, BEGINNING

The Resh is pictured as a "head" or "person." It is the first word of the Bible: *"Breshit;"* = "In the beginning" and for this reason the Hebrew sages used this letter to indicate whatever leads or comes first. Resh means first, or head, as in "Rosh." Rosh Hashanah being the Jewish New Year or the Feast of Trumpets which is the first of the High Holy Days. The head is the highest part of man, containing intellect, reason and wisdom. But Resh is pictured as a bowed head, a mind submitted to God. Christ is the Head of the Church and the firstborn from the dead. (Col 1:18) It can be taken to mean captain, summit, cap stone, first, beginning, best, etc... The 20th Hebrew letter in the Aleph-bet, it has a numerical value of 200.

> *Colossians 1:18 - He is also head of the body, the church; and He is the beginning, the firstborn from the dead, so that He Himself will come to have first place in everything.

ש - SHIN (s,sh) (300) / Meanings:

According to Jewish tradition, the letter *shin* has five definitions (*Ibid.*, pp. 421-424.). The first is *shein*, which means "tooth," or "teeth." The second is *lo shanisi*, meaning "stead-fastness in one's faith." The third is *shinoy*, which is "to change for the good." The fourth is *shuvah*, which means "to return." The fifth is *shanah*, or "year." As a Tooth or teeth. As teeth, it represents eating, consuming, destroying, biting or devouring. In the garden the first sin was associated with fulfilling the desire of the flesh or the mouth. In a positive way it can mean the redemption of the flesh in the consummation of Christ and the figurative feasting on His flesh and blood. It has been taken to mean a sharp tongue (saying sharp, mean words) or the sharpening of one's mind (Deut 6:7). It can represent the Old Covenant Law of retaliation in "an Eye for and eye and a tooth for tooth."

ת - TAV (t) (400) / Meanings: CROSS OR SIGN, PERFECTION, COMPLETION

The Tav means sign, seal, covenant. It is the final letter of the Aleph-bet, symbolizing perfection or Completion. It can represent an impression, mark or seal. In the initial pictograph given by God, the Tav had the shape of a cross. When you make it through the Hebrew Alphabet, you end up at the Cross. - Not an accident! It later evolved into a letter made of the *tav* is a *dalet* and a *nun* - these two letters spell out the name of Dan, דן, one of the tribes of Israel. In the desert, the camp of Dan was the last to proceed. If any of the other tribes left something behind, the tribe of Dan would collect and return it, thus completing their journey and canceling all and any losses. The numerical value of *tav* is four hundred. We find the number four hundred mentioned frequently in the Bible. According to some Jewish mystics, the numerical value of *tav* can represent both the four hundred levels of evil and the four hundred sparks of Godliness that are found in the world. The *tav* thus embodies the ability to transform these negative energies into positive sparks.
   * Abraham needed to buy a burial place for his wife, Sarah. The Torah tells us that he went to Ephron, the leader of the Hittite people, in the city of Hebron and asked him for a piece of land. Ephron responded that he would sell the parcel for four hundred shekels. The name Ephron, עפרן, has the *gematria* of 400: ayin = 70,

pei = 80, *reish* = 200, and *nun* = 50. Significantly, Hebron was the first city in the land of Israel to be officially purchased by the Jewish people.

* The Land of Israel, according to the dimensions in the Torah, measures 400 by 400 *mil* (a *mil* is approximately 1 kilometer).
* The number four hundred is also found pertaining to the "Covenant between the Parts," when God caused Abraham to fall into a deep slumber and told him that his children would reside in a foreign land (the land of Egypt) for four hundred years and afterwards go out with great wealth and an out-stretched arm.

NOTE: It states in the *Talmud* (*Shabbos* 104a.) that the letter *tav* represents the word אמת, *emes*, meaning truth. The reason *emes* is represented by its last letter (*tav*) and not its first (*alef*) is that the essence of truth is determined at the end of a journey or passage, not at the beginning. Often when we begin something, the truth of the matter does not seem attractive. Only upon seeing the outcome do we appreciate that the path of *emes* was the only way to travel. This is the reason for using the *tav* to signify אמת. If the Sages of the *Talmud* needed a letter to symbolize truth, why didn't they pick the א, the first letter of *emes*? Because the letter *tav* represents humankind's ultimate destination, the culmination of our Divine service to perfect the world. And this truth will be unveiled in the final stages of the coming of *Mashiach*.

INTERPRETING THE HEBREW CALENDAR

Just as we keep track of time by a gregorian calendar in the west, many other nations keep time by their own native calendars. Many muslims keep an Islamic Calendar, Indians and Chinese have their own calendars and the Hebrews have their own calendar.

The Hebrews claim to have started counting years starting the year Adam and Eve were created. The Gregorian calendar year 2020, on the Hebrew Calendar will be the year 5780. This is 5780 years from Adam and Eve.

And God said, "Let there be lights in the vault of the sky to separate the day from the night, and let them serve as signs to mark sacred times, and days and years. - Genesis 1:14 (NIV)

According to the passage above, what was God's purpose in separating day and night, creating days and ultimately time itself?

"Now the Lord said to Moses and Aaron in the land of Egypt, ² "This month [Nisan] shall be the beginning of months for you; it is to be the first month of the year to you." - Exodus 12:1-2

According to the passage above, who initiated the Hebrew Monthly Calendar?

Out of all the calendars on the earth, there is only one the Bible validates and claims as being initiated by God. For this reason, we ought to pay close attention to the Hebrew Calendar.

HEBREW NUMERALS

In the system of Hebrew numerals, there is no notation for zero. Each unit (1, 2, ..., 9) is assigned a separate letter, each tens (10, 20, ..., 90) a separate letter, and the first four hundreds (100, 200, 300, 400) a separate letter. The later hundreds (500, 600, 700, 800 and 900) are represented by the sum of two or three letters representing the first four hundreds. To represent numbers from 1,000 to 999,999, the same letters are reused to serve as thousands, tens of thousands, and hundreds of thousands. Gematria (Jewish numerology) uses these transformations extensively.

When specifying years of the Hebrew calendar in the present millennium, writers often simplify things by omitting the "thousands" and deal primarily with the centuries, decades and years. So to write down the Hebrew year 5781 (which is 2021 on the Gregorian calendar), we would waive the 5000, and focus on the 781. 781 written out would be - Tav(400) + Shin(300) = 700, + Peh(80) + Aleph (1).

Many believe God uses the Hebrew calendar as a means to speak prophetically over each new year. For instance, if we take the year 5781 by its word meaning we see that those living during 5781 living during a century of consumerism, a decade of voicing what they've learned, and a year of coming into strength through oneness and unity. This is spelled out below.

* The century of 700 (from Tav (400) which means peoples and/or places) + Shin(300) which means to consume or eat). This is saying that our century is a century where people and places are consuming and being consumed.

* The decade of 80 (from Peh (80) which is the picture of a Mouth. It means Word, expression, vocalization and follows the letter Ayin in the Aleph-Bet so it means to Speak (mouth) after understanding (eyes). It likely symbolizes a year of "speaking [or planning] after obtaining understanding."

* They year of 1 (The pictograph of the Aleph represents an ox. Traditionally it has been taken to mean strength, provider or leader. Means union singleness, or oneness.)

So according to the Hebrew Calendar, the decade between 2020 and 2030 is a decade of "speaking [or planning] after obtaining understanding." It will be one of great wisdom on the earth.

5770s (2010-2020) - A decade of Ayin (Eyes), meaning a decade of breakthrough in knowledge, wisdom and understanding.

5780s (2020-2030) - A decade of Peh (Mouth or Words), meaning a decade of putting language and manifestation to the understanding of Ayin.

5790s (2030-2040) - A decade of Tsade (man reaching up), meaning a decade of reaching or asking for something we realize we don't have. Could signify great need on a global scale.

As you can see, within the Hebrew Aleph-Bet and numeric system lies the potential for a sea of prophetic meaning. Every number and every word carries a potential deeper meaning awaiting discovery.

In the space provided below, please choose a Hebrew year (preferably a soon approaching one) and translate its meaning using the Aleph-Bet letter meanings given in this chapter.

5
GOD SPEAKS THROUGH ANCIENT WORDS

ANCIENT HEBREW WORDS LOST IN TRANSLATION

Although it was written mostly in Greek, the entire New Testament is a work of Hebrew culture. Jesus was a Jew and so were most of His followers. If they were not by birth, then they were by conversion. Almost every concept in the New Testament has Jewish roots. When Hebrew words, ideas and customs are translated into the Greek language, and from there into the English language, entire meanings can be lost.

This is exactly what has happened in much of the Gentile Church. So much of the original word meanings and concepts have been lost in translation. The result is often innocent but ignorant of the real meanings and power of the original.

In this chapter we will look at 33 Hebrew words and concepts the New Testament and New Covenant were founded upon, but whose meanings have since been lost in translation.

33 HEBREW WORDS EVERY BELIEVER SHOULD KNOW

Note: I have used Jeff A. Benner's work through the Ancient Hebrew Research Center as a source for many of the following definitions. All scripture in this chapter is King James Version.

Please highlight the significant things you read about each of these words:

ATONEMENT / KAPHAR: The Hebrew word kaphar means "to cover over" such as a lid and is the word for the lid of the ark of the covenant (though many translations translate this as mercy seat for no etymological reason). This word is translated as "pitch" which was spread over the ark in order to make it water tight (Genesis 6:14) This same word is also translated as a atonement. The word atonement is abstract but in order to understand the true Hebrew meaning of a word we must look to the concrete meaning. If an offense has been made the one that has been offended can act as though the offense is covered over and unseen. We express this idea through the word of forgiveness. Atonement is an outward action that covers over the error.

In many New Testament translations, it is interesting that the word "Atonement" is translated "Reconciliation." What does the following passage tell you about Atonement or Reconciliation?

[17] Therefore if anyone is in Christ, he is a new creature; the old things passed away; behold, new things have come. [18] Now all these things are from God, who reconciled us to Himself through Christ and gave us the ministry of reconciliation, [19] namely, that God was in Christ reconciling the world to Himself, not counting their trespasses against them, and He has committed to us the word of reconciliation. [20] Therefore, we are ambassadors for Christ, as though God were making an appeal through us; we beg you on behalf of Christ, be reconciled to God. [21] He made Him who knew no sin to be sin on our behalf, so that we might become the righteousness of God in Him. - 2 Corinthians 5:17-21

BLESS / BARAK: Every word in the Ancient Hebrew language was related to an image of action, something that could be sensed (as observed by the five senses - seen, heard, smelled, touched or felt) and in motion. The word bless, found numerous times in English translations of the Bible, is a purely abstract word that cannot be sensed, nor is it in motion. In order to interpret this word correctly we must find its original concrete meaning.

As addressed in chapter one, the word "bless" is "barak" in Hebrew. In Genesis 24:11 we read, "And he made the camels "kneel down" outside the city." The phrase "kneel down" is the Hebrew verb ברך (B.R.K), the very same word translated as "bless." The concrete meaning of ברך is to kneel down. It paints a similar picture of the idea of praise and worship. The extended meaning of this word is to pronounce and place credit, honor or value on another. God "blesses" us by providing for our needs and we in turn "bless" God by giving him credit and thanksgiving.

In the New Testament Greek, the word for bless is "eulogeo" which can be interpreted, "praise, celebrate, bless, make happy, or bestow favor." In the passage below, exchange the word "blessed" for the word "celebrated," "happy," or "favored."

[3] *"Blessed are the poor in spirit, for theirs is the kingdom of heaven.* [4] *"Blessed are those who mourn, for they shall be comforted.* [5] *"Blessed are the gentle, for they shall inherit the earth.* [6] *"Blessed are those who hunger and thirst for righteousness, for they shall be satisfied.* [7] *"Blessed are the merciful, for they shall receive mercy.* [8] *"Blessed are the pure in heart, for they shall see God.* [9] *"Blessed are the peacemakers, for they shall be called sons of God.* [10] *"Blessed are those who have been persecuted for the sake of righteousness, for theirs is the kingdom of*

heaven. ¹¹ "Blessed are you when people insult you and persecute you, and falsely say all kinds of evil against you because of Me. ¹² Rejoice and be glad, for your reward in heaven is great; for in the same way they persecuted the prophets who were before you." - Matthew 5:3-11

BREAK / PARAR: While the word keep, as in "keep the commands of God" does not mean obedience but guarding and protecting, the meaning of "break the commands of God" does not mean disobedience. The Hebrew word parar, translated as break, has its pictoral root in the treading of grain on the threshing floor by oxen to open up the hulls to remove the seeds. To the Ancient Hebrews, breaking the commands of God was equated with throwing it on the ground and trampling on it. In both cases, keeping and breaking are related to ones attitude toward the commands. A child who disobeys his parents and is genuinely apologetic shows honor and respect to his parents. But a child who willfully disobeys with no sign of remorse has trampled on his parents teachings and requires discipline. Jesus addresses this concept when He tells the pharisees, *"Have you not read in the Law, that on the Sabbath the priests in the temple break the Sabbath and are innocent?"(Matt 12:5)*. Jesus was saying the outward is different than the inward. They were keeping the Sabbath in their hearts while working with their actions.

This being said, in the New Testament, we see Jesus, the Bread of Life broken on the cross and trampled under foot. To this day, we break the bread and consume it for the same purposes. What does the following passage tell you about the breaking of the body of Jesus.

When He had reclined at the table with them, He took the bread and blessed it, and breaking it, He began giving it to them... They began to relate their experiences on the road and how He was recognized by them in the breaking of the bread. - Luke 24:30-35

COMMAND / MITSVAH: The word command, as well as commandment, is used to translate the Hebrew word mits'vah but does not properly convey the meaning of mits'vah. The word command implies words of force or power as a General commands his troops. The word mits'vah is better understood as a directive. To see the picture painted by this word it is helpful to look at a related word, tsiyon meaning a desert or a landmark. The Ancient Hebrews were a nomadic people who traveled the deserts in search of green pastures for their flocks. A nomad uses the various rivers, mountains, rock outcroppings, etc... as landmarks to give them their direction. The verb form of mits'vah is tsavah meaning to direct one on a journey. The mits'vah of the Bible are not commands, or rules and regulations, they are directives or landmarks that we look for to guide us. The word tsiyon meaning landmark is also the word translated as Zion, the mountain of God but, not just a mountain, it is the landmark.

"Whoever then annuls one of the least of these commandments, and teaches others to do the same, shall be called least in the kingdom of heaven; but whoever keeps and teaches them, he shall be called great in the kingdom of heaven." - Matthew 5:19

According to the passage above, what was Jesus' stance toward the Old Testament commandments?

COVENANT / BERIYT: While the Hebrew word beriyt means "covenant" the cultural background of the word is helpful in understanding its full meaning. Beriyt comes from the parent root word bar meaning grain. Grains were fed to livestock to fatten them up to prepare them for the slaughter. Two other Hebrew words related to beriyt and also derived from the parent root bar can help understand the meaning of beriyt. The word beriy means fat and barut means meat. Notice the common theme with bar, beriy and barut, they all have to do with the slaughtering of livestock. The word beriyt is literally the animal that is slaughtered for the covenant ceremony. The phrase "make a covenant" is found thirteen times in the Hebrew Bible. In the Hebrew text this phrase is "karat beriyt". The word karat literally means "to cut". When a covenant is made a fattened animal is cut into pieces and laid out on the ground. Each party of the covenant then passes through the pieces signifying that if one of the parties fails to meet the agreement then the other has the right to do to the other what they did to the animal (see Genesis 15:10 and Jeremiah 34:18-20).

"[18] I will give the men who have transgressed My covenant, who have not fulfilled the words of the covenant which they made before Me, when they cut the calf in two and passed between its parts— [19] the officials of Judah and the officials of Jerusalem, the court officers and the priests and all the people of the land who passed between the parts of the calf— [20] I will give them into the hand of *their enemies and into the hand of those who seek their life." - Jeremiah 34:18-20*

ETERNITY / OLAM: The ancient Hebrew words that are used to described distance and direction are also used to describe time. The Hebrew word for east is qedem and literally means "the direction of the rising sun". Westerners tend to use north as our major orientation in maps and such, but the Hebrews used the east as the head of the map and all directions are oriented to this direction. For example one of the words for south is teyman from the root yaman meaning "to the right". The word qedem is also the word for the past. In the ancient Hebrew mind the past is in front of you while the future is behind you, the opposite way we think of the past and future. This is because you can see the past but the future is yet unknown. The Hebrew word for eternity, "olam" means in the far distance. When looking off in the far distance it is difficult to make out any details and what is beyond that horizon cannot be seen. This concept is the olam. The word olam is also used for time for the distant past or the distant future as a time that is difficult to know or perceive. This word is frequently translated as eternity or forever but in the English language it is misunderstood to mean a continual span of time that never ends. In the Hebrew mind it is simply what is at or beyond the horizon, a very distant time. A common phrase in the Hebrew is "l'olam va'ed" and is usually translated as "forever and ever" but in the Hebrew it means "to the distant horizon and again" meaning "a very distant time and even further" and is used to express the idea of a very ancient or future time.

In the space provided below each of the following verses, please describe what these passages reveal to you about the idea of eternity:

"And the LORD God said, Behold, the man is become as one of us, to know good and evil: and now, lest he put forth his hand, and take also of the tree of life, and eat, and live forever (olam)." - Genesis 3:22 (KJV)

"There were giants in the earth in those days; and also after that, when the sons of God came in unto the daughters of men, and they bare children to them, the same became mighty men which were of old (olam), men of renown." - Genesis 6:4 (KJV)

For all the land which thou seest, to thee will I give it, and to thy seed forever (olam). - Genesis 13:15 (KJV)

And I will establish my covenant between me and thee and thy seed after thee in their generations for an everlasting (olam) covenant, to be a God unto thee, and to thy seed after thee. - Genesis 17:7 (KJV)

FACE / PANIYM: The Hebrew word פנים (paniym) is a plural noun meaning "face." As the Hebrew language expresses the idea of motion in most words, this plural noun conveys the ideas of mood, emotions and thoughts, the different motions reflected in the face. This Hebrew word more precisely means the "presence" or the "wholeness of being" of an individual.

"For if you return to the Lord, your brothers and your sons will find compassion before those who led them captive and will return to this land. For the Lord your God is gracious and compassionate, and will not turn His face away from you if you return to Him." - 2 Chronicles 30:9

After understanding the Hebrew concept of "face," what does the passage above reveal to you?

FAITH / EMUNAH: The Hebrew root aman means firm, something that is supported or secure. This word is used in Isaiah 22:23 for a nail that is hammered into a "secure" place. Derived from this root is the word emun meaning a craftsman. A craftsman is one who is firm and secure in his talent. Also derived from aman is the word emunah meaning firmness, something or someone that is firm in their actions. When the Hebrew word emunah is translated as faith, misconceptions of its meaning occur. Faith is usually perceived as a knowing while the Hebrew emunah is a firm action. To have faith in God is not knowing that God exists or knowing that he will act, rather it is that the one with emunah will act with firmness and confidence toward God's will.

"And he believed (emunah) in the LORD; and he counted it to him for righteousness." - Genesis 15:6

"My servant Moses is not so, who is faithful (emunah) in all mine house." - Numbers 12:7

After understanding the Hebrew concept of "Faith," what do the passages above reveal to you?

FEAR / YIRAH: The root meaning of the word yara is "to flow" and is related to words meaning rain or stream as a flowing of water. In Hebrew thought fear can be what is felt when in danger or what is felt when in the presence of an awesome sight or person of great authority. These feelings flow out of the person in such as actions as shaking when in fear or bowing down in awe of one in authority.

"And Moses said unto the people, Fear (yare) not: for God is come to prove you, and that His fear (yirah) may be before your faces, that ye sin not." - Exodus 20:20

FIRMAMENT / RAQIYA: The word raqiya comes from the root word raqa which can be found in several passages including Isaiah 40:19 - "The idol! a workman casts it, and a goldsmith overlays it with gold, and casts for it silver chains." The word "overlay" is the verb root raqa. Raqa is the process of hammering out a piece of gold or other metal into thin plates which was then applied to a carved or molten image. Numbers 16:39 reads "So Eleazar the priest took the bronze censers, which those who were burned had offered; and they were hammered out as a covering for the altar." Here, the phrase "were hammered out" is again the verb root raqa. The gold was hammered into thin sheets then laid over the surface of the alter. The word raqiya is the noun form of the verb raqa and is literally a "hammered out sheet". There are some scientists who have speculated that before the flood there was a thick sheet of water surrounding the earth up in the atmosphere. It is then possible that the "floodgates of heaven were opened," at the beginning of the flood, is the collapse of this "hammered out sheet" of water. It is estimated that the sheet of water would have filtered out harmful sun rays and contributed to the longevity of life on earth before the flood.

"And God said, Let there be a firmament in the midst of the waters, and let it divide the waters from the waters. And God made the firmament, and divided the waters which were under the firmament from the waters which were above the firmament: and it was so. And God called the firmament Heaven. And the evening and the morning were the second day." - Genesis 1:6-8

After understanding the Hebrew concept of "Firmament," what does the passage above reveal to you?

FRINGE / TSIYTSIYT: In Numbers 15:38-40 God commands Israel to put fringes (tsiytsiy in Hebrew) on the corner of their clothes so that they will remember to do the commands of the torah. As the Hebrew mind focuses on the concrete, God uses physical things as reminders and associations for non-physical things. In this case the fringes are reminders of the commands. The word tsiytsiyt is derived from the root tsiyts meaning a blossom. A blossom is a flower that grows on a tree and is the beginning of the fruit. Just as the blossom turns into a fruit, the fringes on the Hebrews garments are also there to bring about fruit in the sense of doing the commands. This is another pictorial lesson teaching that as we let the flower of God's law grow in our hearts, it will produce the fruit of His Spirit.

"Hear, O earth: behold, I will bring evil upon this people, even the fruit of their thoughts, because they have not hearkened unto my words, nor to my law, but rejected it." - Jeremiah 6:19

What warning does the passage above offer us about the fruit of rejecting God's words?

GLORY / KAVOD: In Exodus 16:7 we read "and in the morning you shall see the glory of the LORD" (RSV). What is the "glory" of YHWH? First we must recognize that the "glory" is something that will be seen. Secondly, the word "glory" is an abstract word. If we look at how this word is paralleled with other words in poetical passages of the Bible, we can discover the original concrete meaning of this word. In Psalm 3:3 the kavod of God is paralleled with his shield and in Job 29:20 Job's kavod is paralleled with his bow. In Psalm 24:8 we read "who is this king of the kavod, YHWH is strong and mighty, YHWH is mighty in battle." The original concrete meaning of kavod is battle armaments. This meaning of "armament" fits with the literal meaning of the root of kavod which is "heavy" or "weighty" as armaments are the heavy weapons and defenses of battle. In the Exodus 16:7, Israel will "see" the "armament" of YHWH, who is the one who has done battle for them with the Egyptians.

We can also learn a lot about this word as we study the idea of weight. Weight tells you how much something weighs compared to something else. "Glory" is therefore revealed when the weight or worth of something is made manifest.

GOD / EL, ELO'AH: There are two Hebrew words commonly translated as God, El and Elo'ah. When reading the Bible it is better to have an Ancient Hebrew perception of God rather than our modern western view. The word el was originally written with two pictographic letters, one being an ox head and the other a shepherd staff. The ox represented strength and the staff of the shepherd represented authority. First, the Ancient Hebrews saw God as the strong one of authority. The shepherd staff was also understood as a staff on the shoulders, a yoke. Secondly, the Ancient Hebrews saw God as the ox in the yoke. When plowing a field two oxen were placed in a yoke, one was the older and more experienced and the other the younger and less experienced and the younger would learn from the older. The Hebrews saw God as the older experienced ox and they as the younger who learns from him. The plural form of elo'ah is elohiym and is often translated as God. While English plurals only identify quantity, as in more than one, the Hebrew plural can identify quantity as well as quality. Something that is of great size or stature can be written in the plural form and in this case, God, as the great strength and authority is frequently written in the plural form elohiym. The two letters in these Hebrew words are the ox head representing strength and the shepherd staff representing authority. Combined they mean "the strong authority" as well as "the ox with a staff" (a yoke is understood as a staff on the shoulders).

Does this affect your concept of God? Why?

GOOD / TOV: What does "good" mean? The first use of this word is in Genesis chapter one where God calls his handiwork "good". It should always be remembered that the Hebrews often relate descriptions to functionality. The word tov would best be translated with the word "functional" as it is less an issue of morality and more an issue of functionality. When God looked at His handiwork He did not see that it was "good", He saw that it was functional, kind of like a well oiled and tuned machine. In contrast to this word is the Hebrew word "ra". These two words, tov and ra are used for the tree of the knowledge of "good" and "evil". While "ra" is often translated as evil it is best translated as "dysfunctional".

Understanding the Hebrew concept of good and evil should help us have a healthier view of the law and commands of God as He is less interested in us being right or wrong as He is in our functioning according to our design, purpose and health.

How does this knowledge affect the way you think of good and evil or right and wrong?

How might this knowledge be applied to controversial subjects like homosexuality?

GOOD NEWS / BASAR: The Hebrew word for Good news, or gospel, is basar. This word actually has two meanings, good news and flesh. What does good news and flesh have in common? Flesh, or meat, was only eaten on very special occasions, a feast, the arrival of guests or whenever an event occurs that requires a celebration. As you can see these times of good news were associated with the slaughter of an animal and a meal of flesh.

Understanding the Hebrew concept of the good news as flesh, speaks to the heart of the Gospel, "the Word became flesh and dwelt among us!" (John 1:14) Jesus became the son of man to reveal to the sons of men that they were truly the sons of God. He revealed God's union with our flesh - that our flesh wasn't intrinsically evil, but in fact it was made very good. The incarnation is the core teaching of Christianity. Starting with the gnostics, almost every heresy has had a problem with the incarnation.

How does this affect the way you might preach the gospel?

GRACIOUS / HANAN: The verb חנן (Hh.N.N) is often translated as "to be gracious" or "have mercy," however these are abstract terms and do not help us understand the meaning of this verb from an Hebraic perspective, which always relates words to something concrete. One of the best tools to use to find the more concrete meaning of a word is to look at how that word is paralleled with other words in poetical passages. In the book of Psalms the word חנן is paralleled with "heal," "help," "raise up," "refuge" and "give strength." From a concrete Hebraic perspective, חנן means all of this, and no English word can convey the meaning of the Hebrew, but we could sum up its meaning with "providing protection." Where would a nomadic Hebrew run for protection? The camp, which in the Hebrew language is the word מחנה (mahhaneh, Strong's # 4264), a noun related to חנן.

"And it shall come to pass, when he crieth unto me, that I will hear; for I am gracious." - Exodus 22:27

HEART / LEV: Here is an example of our modern western culture still using a concrete object to express an abstract idea. We often associate the heart with emotions such as love and kindness as in "He has a good heart". This is also true with the Hebrews who saw the heart as the seat of emotion. But unlike us they also saw the heart as the seat of thought whereas we see the brain as the seat of thought. To the ancient Hebrews the heart was the mind including all thoughts and emotions. When we are told to love God with all our heart (Deut 6:5) it is not speaking of an emotional love but to keep our emotions and all our thoughts working for him. The first picture in this Hebrew word is a shepherd staff and represents authority as the shepherd has authority over his flock. The second letter is the picture of the floor plan of the nomadic tent and represents the idea of being inside as the family resides within the tent. When combined they mean "the authority within".

"And GOD saw that the wickedness of man was great in the earth, and that every imagination of the thoughts of his heart was only evil continually." - Genesis 6:5

HOLY / QADOSH: When we use the word holy, as in a holy person, we usually associate this with a righteous or pious person. If we use this concept when interpreting the word holy in the Hebrew Bible then we are misreading the text as this is not the meaning of the Hebrew word qadosh. Qadosh literally means "to be set apart for a special purpose". A related word, qedesh, is one who is also set apart for a special purpose but not in the same way we think of "holy" but is a male prostitute (Deut 23:17). Israel was qadosh because they were separated from the other nations as servants of God. The furnishings in the tabernacle were qadosh as they were not to be used for anything except for the work in the tabernacle. While we may not think of ourselves as "holy" we are in fact set apart from the world to be God's servants and representatives.

As we can see the word holy has less to do with moral purity and more to do with calling and consecration. The calling and consecration might be one of moral purity, but the point is that the object of holiness has now been devoted to that which it was set apart to do.

How does this knowledge affect your view of holiness?

KEEP / SHAMAR: Many times I have heard it said that no one can keep all of the commands but, this is not true. From an Hebraic perspective of the word shamar behind the English word keep, it is possible to keep all of the commands. The problem lies in our understanding of keep as meaning obedience, but this is not the meaning of shamar. It should first be recognized that not all of the commands of the torah are for all people. Some are only for the priests, some are only for men and some are only for women. Some are only for children and some are for leaders. But, it should also be understood that even if a command is not for you, you can still keep it. The original picture painted by the Hebrew word shamar is a sheepfold. When a shepherd was out in the wilderness with his flock, he would gather thorn bushes to erect a corral to place his flock in at night. The thorns would deter predators and thereby protect and guard the sheep from harm. The word shamiyr derived from this root means a thorn. The word shamar means to guard and protect and can be seen in the Aaronic blessing, May Yahweh bless you and keep (guard and protect) you. One keeps the commands of God by guarding and protecting them.

How does this knowledge affect your view of keeping God's word?

LAW / TORAH: To interpret the Hebrew word torah as law is about the same as interpreting the word father as disciplinarian. While the father is a disciplinarian he is much more and in the same way torah is much more than law. The word torah is derived from the root yarah meaning to throw. This can be any kind of throwing such as a rock or an arrow from the bow or throwing the finger in a direction to point something out. Another word derived from this root is the word moreh which can mean and archer, one who throws the arrow, or a teacher, as one who points the way. The word torah is literally the teachings of the teacher or parent. When a parent is teaching a child a new task and he demonstrates a willingness to learn but fails to grasp the teaching completely the parent does not punish the child but rather encourages and builds on the teaching. In contrast to this a law is a set of rules that if not observed correctly will result in punishment and there is no room for teaching. The torah of God are his teachings to his children which are given in love to encourage and strengthen.

"Then said the LORD unto Moses, Behold, I will rain bread from heaven for you; and the people shall go

out and gather a certain rate every day, that I may prove them, whether they will walk in my law, or no." - Exodus 16:4

How does this understanding of the law affest the way you might read the passage above?

LIFE / HHAI: The Hebrew word hhai is usually translated as life. In the Hebrew language all words are related to something concrete or physical, something that can be observed by one of the five senses. Some examples of concrete words would be tree, water, hot, sweet or loud. The western Greek mind frequently uses abstracts or mental words to convey ideas. An abstract word is something that cannot be sensed by the five senses. Some examples would be bless, believe, and the word life. Whenever working with an abstract word in the Biblical text it will help to uncover the concrete background to the word for proper interpretation. How did the ancient Hebrew perceive "life". A clue can be found in Job 38:39, "Will you hunt prey for the lion and will you fill the stomach of the young lion?". In this verse the word "stomach" is the Hebrew word hhai. In our culture it is very uncommon for anyone to experience true hunger but this was an all too often experience for the Ancient Hebrews. To the Ancient Hebrews life is seen as a full stomach while an empty stomach is seen as death.

LOVE / AHAV: We do not choose our parents or siblings but are instead given to us as a gift from above, a privileged gift. Even in the ancient Hebrew culture ones wife was chosen for you. It is our responsibility to provide and protect that privileged gift. In our modern Western culture love is an abstract thought of emotion, how one feels toward another but the Hebrew meaning goes much deeper. As a verb this word means "to provide and protect what is given as a privilege" as well as " to have an intimacy of action and emotion". We are told to love God and our neighbors, not in an emotional sense, but in the sense of our actions.

How does this understanding of love affect the way you might read the greatest commandment, "And thou shalt love the LORD thy God with all thine heart, and with all thy soul, and with all thy might." - Deuteronomy 6:5?

MESSIAH / MESHI'AHH: The word Messiah is a transliteration of the Hebrew word meshiahh (meh-shee-ahh - the "hh" is pronounced hard like the "ch" in the name Bach). This word comes from the root mashahh meaning "to smear" as in Jeremiah 22:14 where it is usually translated as "painted". In the ancient world olive oil was a very versatile commodity. It was used in cooking as well as a medicine as it is a disinfectant, no shepherd was without a flask of olive oil which he smeared on his or his sheep's injuries. The verb mashahh is also translated as "anointed", as in Exodus 29:7, in the sense of smearing olive oil on the head. This ceremony was performed on anyone becoming a King, Priest or Prophet in the service of Yahweh. From the root mashahh comes the noun meshiahh literally meaning "one who is smeared with olive oil for office of authority" or, as it is usually translated, "anointed". This word is also used for any "one who holds an office of authority" (such as a king or priest) even if that person was not ceremonially smeared with oil. A good example of this is Cyrus, the King of Persia. While he was not ceremonially smeared with oil, he was one of authority who served Yahweh through his decree allowing Israel to return to Jerusalem.

How does this knowledge affect your view of the word Messiah or Christ?

NAME / SHEM: When we see a name such as "King David" we see the word "King" as a title and "David" as a name. In our western mind a title describes a character trait while a name is simply an identifier. In the Hebrew language there is no such distinction between names and titles. Both words, King and David, are descriptions of character traits, King is "one who reigns" while David is "one who is loved". It is also common to identify the word "Elohiym" (God) as a title and YHWH (Yahweh, the LORD, Jehovah) as a name. What we do not realize is that both of these are character traits, YHWH meaning "the one who exists" and Elohiym is "one who has power and authority". The Hebrew word "shem" more literally means "character". When the Bible speaks of taking God's name to the nations, he is not talking about the name itself but his character. When the command to not take God's name in vain literally means not to represent his character in a false manner. It is similar to our expression of "having a good name" which is not about the name itself but the character of the one with that name.

How does this knowledge affect the way you read the following passages?

"And he called his name Noah, saying, This same shall comfort us concerning our work and toil of our hands..." Genesis 5:29

"Unto the place of the altar, which he had made there at the first: and there Abram called on the name of the LORD." - Genesis 13:4

"And she called the name of the LORD that spake unto her, Thou God seest me: for she said, Have I also here looked after him that seeth me?" - Genesis 16:13

PEACE / SHALOM: The noun שלום (shalom), often translated as "peace," comes from the verb שלם (Sh.L.M). The verb shalam means to "restore" in the sense of replacing or providing what is needed in order to make someone or something whole and complete. The noun שלום (shalom) is one who has, or has been provided, what is needed to be whole and complete.

This Hebrew definition of the word "shalom" is in direct correlation with the New Testament Greek idea of "salvation" which literally is "sozo" meaning wholeness. The Greek "sozo" or "a restoration of wholeness" is the result of the Hebrew "Shalom."

"And the peace of God, which passeth all understanding, shall keep your hearts and minds through Christ Jesus." - Philippians 4:7

PRAISE / HALEL: The word praise is an abstract word that has no relationship with the ancient Hebrew's concrete way of thinking. While the word halel is translated as "praise" it is also translated as "shine" as in Job 29:3. The original meaning of halel is the North Star. This star, unlike all of the other stars, remains motionless and constantly shines in the northern sky and is used as a guide when traveling. In the Ancient Hebrew mind we praise God by looking at him as the guiding star that shines to show us our direction. The first letter in this Hebrew word (from right to left) is a picture of a man with his arms raised up as pointing toward something of greatness. The second two letters are pictures of a shepherd staff which is used by the shepherd to move his flock toward a direction. When these two letters are combined the idea of looking toward something is formed.

"Stand every morning to thank and praise the LORD, and likewise at evening..." - 1 Chronicles 23:30

PRAY / PALAL: In our modern religious culture prayer is a communication between man and God. While this definition could be applied to some passage of the Bible (such as Genesis 20:17) it is not an Hebraic definition of the Hebrew word palal. By looking at the etymology of this word we can better see the Hebraic meaning. The word palal comes from the parent root pal meaning "fall" (The root pal is most likely the root of our word fall which can etymologically be written as phal). Pal is also the root of the Hebrew word naphal also meaning "fall". The word palal literally means to "fall down to the ground in the presence of one in authority pleading a cause." This can be seen in Isaiah 45:14 where the Sabeans fall down and make supplication (this is the Hebrew word palal) to Cyrus.

"Thus saith the LORD, The labour of Egypt, and merchandise of Ethiopia and of the Sabeans... and they shall fall down unto thee, they shall make supplication unto thee, saying, Surely God is in thee; and there is none else, there is no God." - Isaiah 45:14

PRIEST / KOHEN: While the priests of Israel were the religious leaders of the community this is not the meaning of the word kohen. The Hebrew word for the priests of other nations is komer from a root meaning burn and may be in reference to the priests who burn children in the fires of Molech (2 Kings 23:10). The word kohen comes from a root meaning a base such as the base of a column. The koheniym (plural of kohen) are the structure support of the community. It is their responsibility to keep the community standing tall and straight, a sign of righteousness.

"Jesus Christ, who... hath made us kings and priests unto God and his Father; to him be glory and dominion for ever and ever. Amen." - Revelation 1:5-6

How does this knowledge affect the way you read the passage above?

RIGHTEOUS / TSADIYQ: What is a righteous person? The word righteous is an abstract word and in order to understand this word from an Hebraic mindset we must uncover its original concrete meaning. One of the best ways to determine the original concrete meaning of a word is to find it being used in a sentence where its concrete meaning can be seen. For example the word yashar is usually translated as upright or righteous (abstracts) but is also translated as "straight". From this we can conclude that a "yashar" is one who walks a straight line. The problem with the word tsadiyq, and its verb form tsadaq, is that there are no uses of this word in its concrete meaning. The next method is to compare how the word in question is paralleled with other Hebrew words as commonly found in the poetical passages of the Bible. Sometimes these parallels will be synonyms and other times antonyms. When we look at the word tsadiyq we find that it is commonly paralleled with the word "rasha". Rasha is usually translated as "wicked" but has a concrete meaning of "to depart from the path and become lost". From this we can conclude that a tsadiyq is one who remains on the path. The path is the course through life which God has outlined for us in his word.

This understanding carries over into the New Testament as the word "righteous" and the word "sinner" are used as antonyms throughout. Many evangelical churches have forgotten this important truth as their church services are set up to preach to "sinners" instead of to "righteous" believers. Because of this, many evangelicals are convinced they are still sinners instead of the righteousness of God in Christ. You cannot be a sinner and be righteous at the same time. Likewise you cannot be righteous and a sinner at the same time.

How does this knowledge affect the way you read the following passages?

"I have not come to call the righteous but sinners to repentance." Luke 5:32 (NASB)

"Having been freed from sin, you became slaves of righteousness." Romans 6:18 (NASB)

"He made Him who knew no sin to be sin on our behalf, so that we might become the righteousness of God in Him." - 2 Corinthians 5:21 (NASB)

SHINE / OR: The word אור (or), as a noun means "light" and as a verb, it means to "give light" or "shine." It is also related to the idea of bringing order, in the same way that you bring about order in the darkness when you turn on the lights.

SPIRIT / RU'AHH: The Hebrew word ru'ach literally means the wind and is derived from the parent root rach a prescribed path. The word rach is not found in the Biblical text but defined by the various child roots derived from it. The child roots derived from this parent root are arach, rachah and yarach. Arach is a traveler who follows a prescribed path from one place to another. Rachah is a millstone which goes round and round in the sense of following a prescribed path to crush grain into flour. Yarach is the root of yere'ach meaning the moon which follows a prescribed path in the night sky. The child root ru'ach is literally the wind that follows a prescribed path each season. By extension ru'ach means the wind of a man or what is usually translated as spirit. A man's wind is not just a spiritual entity within a man but is understood by the Ancient Hebrews as his character.

In Greek, the word for spirit is "pneuma" which is the word for wind or breath. Wind has to move to exist. Its movement defines it, just like the Hebrew word, this caries the idea of moving on a course.

How does this knowledge affect the way you read the following passages?

"Just then there was a man in their synagogue with an unclean spirit; and he cried out..." - Mark 1:23

"The wind blows where it wishes and you hear the sound of it, but do not know where it comes from and where it is going; so is everyone who is born of the Spirit." - John 3:8

"...for John baptized with water, but you will be baptized with the Holy Spirit not many days from now." - Acts 1:5

"This man had been instructed in the way of the Lord; and being fervent in spirit, he was speaking and teaching accurately the things concerning Jesus, being acquainted only with the baptism of John." - Acts 18:25

TRUTH / EMET: The root of this word is aman, a word often translated as "believe" but more literally means "support" as we see in Isaiah 22:23 where it says "I will drive him like a peg in a place of support..." A belief in God is not a mental exercise of knowing that God exists but rather our responsibility to show him our support. The word "emet" has the similar meaning of firmness, something that is firmly set in place. Psalmes 119:142 says, "the 'Torah' (the teachings of God) is 'emet' (set firmly in place).

*"So Jesus was saying to those Jews who had believed Him, "If you continue in My word, then you are truly disciples of Mine; and you will know the

truth, and the truth will make you free." - *John 8:31-32*

How does this knowledge affect the way you read the passage above?

WILDERNESS / MIDVAR: For forty years God had Israel wander in the 'wilderness'. Insights into why God had chosen the wilderness for their wanderings can be found in the roots of this word. The root word is 'davar' and is most frequently translated as a thing or a word. The original picture painted by this word to the Hebrews is the arrangement of things to create order. Speech is an ordered arrangement of words. In the ancient Hebrew mind words are 'things' and are just as 'real' as food or other 'thing'. When a word is spoken to another it is 'placed in the ears' no different than when food is given to another it is 'placed in the mouth'. The Hebrew name Devorah (Deborah) means 'bee' and is the feminine form of the word davar. Bees are a community of insects which live in a perfectly ordered arrangement. The word 'midvar' meaning wilderness is actually a place that exists as a perfectly arranged order as its ecosystem is in harmony and balance. By placing Israel in this environment he is teaching them balance, order and harmony.

WORSHIP / SHAHHAH: In our modern western culture worship is an action directed toward God and God alone. But this is not the case in the Hebrew Bible. The word shehhah is a common Hebrew word meaning to prostrate oneself before another in respect. We see Moses doing this to his father in law in Exodus 18:7. When the translators translate the word shehhah they will use the word "worship" when the bowing down is directed toward God but as "obeisance" or other equivalent word when directed toward another man. There is no Hebrew word meaning worship in the sense that we are used to using it in our culture today. From an Hebraic perspective worship, or shehhah is the act of getting down on ones knees and placing the face down on the ground before another worthy of respect.

"Then the man bowed low and worshiped the Lord." - Genesis 24:26

FOUNDATIONS FOR UNDERSTANDING GOD

As you might be thinking, many of these words are used on a daily basis in Christian circles yet their biblical meaning is often completely misunderstood. To understand the way God speaks it helps to understand the ways in which He has spoken.

In this chapter, we learned the definitions of these foundational words, but perhaps more importantly, we hopefully began to grasp some of the ways the Eastern, Hebrew language and concepts might differ foundationally from ours. Understanding the way the Hebrew mind and language worked gives us great insight into the mind and teachings of Christ. Understanding the definitions of these elemental Hebrew words offers us a humble foundation for worshipping God in spirit and in truth.

6
HE SPEAKS THROUGH HIS FEASTS

GOD'S FEASTS

When parents have something important to communicate or announce to their children, like the arrival of a new baby brother or sister, the death of a grandparent, or a change in career, home or lifestyle, they might plan a special day to give that event the proper time needed to communicate in a manner worthy of the event. Sometimes these days become marked as birthdays or memorial days that are observed each year as a way to honor the life of person or thing the day is dedicated to. In the same way, God has established seven Holy days and He continues to use these days to communicate to us about what He has done in the past and what He plans to do in the future.

The Hebrew word for "feasts" (*moadim*) literally means "appointed times." God has carefully planned and appointed the times of each of these seven feasts to reveal to us a special story. Just as God speaks through the Hebrew language and calendar, He also speaks to us every year through the feasts. When Israel first became a nation, God told Moses to have the nation observe seven national holidays. Each year to this day, these feasts act as both a testimony to what God has already done as well as a prophetic foretelling of what He will one day do. The feasts are laden with meaning and God continues to use them to communicate corporately and personally to this day.

"And the LORD spoke to Moses, saying, "Speak to the children of Israel, and say to them: 'The feasts of

the LORD, which you shall proclaim to be holy convocations, these are My feasts." (Lev 23:1-2)

According to the passage above, whose feasts were they?

THE EARLY CHURCH OBSERVED THE FEASTS

Notice, He did not say these were the feast of the Jews or the feasts of the Christians but "the feast of the Lord." They are memorial days that both Christians and Jews have good cause to celebrate. These festivals were instituted by our Father in the first testament and reaffirmed by Jesus in the new testament.

In each of the following passages, please highlight the portions of text that show whether or not the early Church observed the Jewish feasts.

"[Jesus] said to them, 'With fervent desire I have desired to eat this Passover with you before I suffer'" - Luke 22:15

"For Christ our Passover also has been sacrificed. Therefore let us celebrate the feast..." - I Corinthians 5:7-8

"....I must by all means keep this feast that cometh in Jerusalem.. .." - Acts 18:21 (KJV)

"For Paul had determined to sail by Ephesus, because he would not spend the time in Asia: for he hasted, if it were possible for him, to be at Jerusalem the day of Pentecost." - Acts 20:16

"But I will tarry at Ephesus until Pentecost." - 1 Corinthians 16:8

As you can see from the passages above, Jesus, Paul and the first century Church observed the feasts of Israel. This being said, the early Church did not consider it mandatory for Gentiles to observe them. The early Church debated as to how much of the Old Covenant the New Covenant believers were to observe. These debates ranged from those who wanted to scrap the entire Old Covenant all together to those who wanted to continue in all of it. What ended up happening was most Jewish believers continued to observe the feasts while releasing the rest of the Church to obey their own consciences regarding the matter.

"Therefore, let no one judge you because of what you eat or drink or about the observance of annual holy days, New Moon Festivals, or weekly worship days. [17] These are a shadow of the things to come, but the body that casts the shadow belongs to Christ." - Colossians 2:16-17

While it is not mandatory for believers to observe the feasts, there is infinitely more meaning for the Christian observance of the feasts than for the Jewish observance of the feasts. After all, Christ is the substance of the feasts and the feasts were all merely foreshadows of Him. Sadly, many Christians have become more observant of pagan holidays like easter and halloween than they are with the Judeo-Christian biblical holy-days like Tabernacles, Passover and Pentecost.

Observing the feasts ought to serve as enlightening and celebratory events that bring revelation and life to those who observe them.

There can be tremendous purpose for the corporate body to continue to observe them, or at least maintain awareness of their times and meanings as God has promised to use the feasts to perform special events in the future. If we stop observing the feasts then we might not recognize what God is doing when these events occur.

This chapter will serve as an introduction to the feasts and how God might speak to you through them. This chapter will not focus on the details of how to observe the feasts (You can look it up and do it on your own or join a group if you'd like to), instead, this chapter will focus on the bigger picture an overall prophetic purpose of these feasts through History. We will merely open the door to the treasure trove of wealth, it will be your job to enter the room and partake if you so desire.

GOD SPEAKS THROUGH HIS FEASTS

The first three of the Feasts of Israel are in the springtime. One is in the summer and three are in the fall. All seven of these holy days, (from which we get our word 'holiday'), are special occasions in which God calls His people aside. The seven Feasts of Israel are not merely religious festivals of a bygone era. They are rehearsals of things to come and memorials of things that have happened in times past. They are appointed days when God has promised repeated visitation with man. One of the universal ways God has chosen to speak to mankind is through these "appointed times." Our God is not idle. He is hard at work on a continuing seven part project. Step by step the God of Israel is establishing and releasing waves of truth upon the evolving mind of His people. We are going from glory to glory and from faith to faith. The feasts are signposts guiding us on this pilgrimage. These Seven Feasts are not just "religion". They are days of past and future glory on the calendar of the Cosmos. They are marks on a roadmap that runs from the garden of Eden, to the Exodus of Moses, to the Passion of Jesus to the final consummation at the end of the Age.

Many Christian Scholars agree that the first four feasts that have been fulfilled and the fulfillment of the final three feasts is eminent. In these seven feasts God's people learn God's plan for the ages. His agenda for the redemption of man and the restoration of the cosmos has already been set. It was decreed in heaven from before time began. Things on this planet may be in a mess right now, but that will not always be the case. God will step into history again. He will surprise us again just as He has done in the past. He has an ongoing program. God's agenda is in full operation and right on schedule. Four feasts are down. Three fall feasts are yet to come.

The prophet Amos records that God declared He would do nothing without first revealing it to His servants, the prophets (Amos 3:7). If the prophets of today are going to understand His greater timing for the earth, they will need to understand His "appointed times." From the Old Covenant to the New, Genesis to Revelation, many of the prophecies made by the prophets were merely revelations that came as the prophets observed and understood the purposes of God's feasts. God has a seven step program for the age of man and it is revealed in the Jewish feasts of Leviticus 23.

A large portion of Leviticus 23 is given below. Please highlight the seven feasts mentioned in the passage.

The Lord spoke to Moses, ² "Tell the Israelites: These are the appointed festivals with the Lord, which you must announce as holy assemblies. ³ You may work for six days. But the seventh day is a day of worship, a day when you don't work, a holy assembly. Don't do any work. It is the Lord's day of worship wherever you live. ⁴ "The following are the Lord's appointed festivals with holy assemblies, which you must announce at their appointed times.

SPRING FESTIVALS OVERVIEW
⁵ "The fourteenth day of the first month, in the evening, is the Lord's Passover. ⁶ The fifteenth day of this same month is the Lord's Festival of Unleavened Bread. For seven days you must eat unleavened bread. ⁷ On the first day there will be a holy assembly. Don't do any regular work. ⁸ Bring the Lord a sacrifice by fire for seven days. On the seventh day there will be a holy assembly. Don't do any regular work." ⁹ The Lord spoke to Moses, ¹⁰ "Tell the Israelites: When you come to the land I am going to give you and you harvest grain, bring the priest a bundle of the first grain you harvest [First Fruits]. ¹¹ He will present it to the Lord so that you will be accepted. He will present it on the day after Passover.... ¹⁵ "Count seven full weeks from the day after Passover (the day you bring the bundle of grain as an offering presented to the Lord) ¹⁶ until the day after the seventh week. This is a total of fifty days. Then bring a new grain offering to the Lord [Pentecost]... ²¹ It is a permanent law for generations to come wherever you live.

FALL FESTIVALS OVERVIEW

[23]{.sup} The Lord spoke to Moses, [24]{.sup} "Tell the Israelites: On the first day of the seventh month hold a worship festival. It will be a memorial day, a holy assembly announced by the blowing of rams' horns [Trumpets]. [25]{.sup} Don't do any regular work. Bring a sacrifice by fire to the Lord." [26]{.sup} The Lord spoke to Moses, [27]{.sup} ' In addition, the tenth day of this seventh month is a special day for the payment for sins [Atonement]. There will be a holy assembly. Humble yourselves, and bring the Lord a sacrifice by fire. [28]{.sup} Don't do any work that day. It is a special day for the payment for sins. It is a time when you make peace with the Lord your God... It is a permanent law for generations to come wherever you live.... [33]{.sup} The Lord spoke to Moses, [34]{.sup} "Tell the Israelites: The fifteenth day of this seventh month is the Festival of Booths to the Lord. It will last seven days. [35]{.sup} On the first day there will be a holy assembly. Don't do any regular work. [36]{.sup} For seven consecutive days bring a sacrifice by fire to the Lord. On the eighth day there will be a holy assembly. Bring the Lord a sacrifice by fire. This is the last festival of the year. Don't do any regular work. [37]{.sup} "These are the Lord's appointed festivals. Announce them as holy assemblies for bringing sacrifices by fire to the Lord. Bring burnt offerings, grain offerings, other sacrifices, and wine offerings—each one on its special day. [38]{.sup} This is in addition to the Lord's days of worship, your gifts, all your vows, and your freewill offerings to the Lord.

In the diagram above, you can see how the Hebrew calendar compares to the Western Gregorian calendar. Notice the three feasts of Spring, Pentecost, and the three of Fall.

THE SPRING FEASTS AS FULFILLED IN CHRIST

The first three of the feasts, the Spring feasts, run back to back over three days. They are Passover, Unleavened Bread and First Fruits. Passover starts Nisan 14 and ends the next day, Unleavened Bread starts Nisan 15 and ends one week later and First Fruits starts Nisan 16 and ends the next day.

There is such meaning to be found in the practice of the rituals of each of these feasts, however, our goal will not be to discover and define all of the details but to offer an overview of each feast's purpose in God, origin in Adam, manifestation in Israel, fulfillment in the incarnation of Christ, application in us and ultimate future in the second coming.

FEAST OF PASSOVER / DEATH

Many Gentiles might be more familiar with the pagan holiday of Easter than they are with the Judeo-Christian holiday of Passover, which both occur around the same time each year.

PASSOVER FROM ADAM AND EVE
Passover is all about how God is chooses to pass over our sins. Like all the feasts, it has its roots in the garden of Eden. Before Adam and Eve sinned and ate from the tree of knowledge of good and evil, Adam was told by God, "do not eat from the tree of the knowledge of good and evil for if you do, in that day you will surely die." (Gen. 2:17) When Adam and Eve sinned, they created a mutant named Death. Death was conceived by sin (James 1:15). The wages of sin is death (Rom 6:23). When Adam and Eve introduced the mutations of

sin and death into God's creation, God had a plan of redemption for the creation. It was called passover.

PASSOVER REPRESENTS FREEDOM FROM CAPTIVITY
Passover was the first feast of the seven mentioned in Leviticus 23 and is New Year's Day for Israel and for the Church. Humanity became enslaved to sin and death in the garden of Eden. Our spiritual slavery as the human race was illustrated as the people of Israel endured their enslavement to Egypt. The Israelites continued as slaves until Moses, being sent by God, liberated them, thus serving as a portrait of what Christ would later do for us all. Passover represents the last day of Israel's captivity and slavery to Egypt and the first day of their new life as a people. This day also represents the last day of our captivity and slavery to sin and death and the first day of our new life as a people as it was on the day of Passover that Christ crucified sn and canceled our debt to death as a race.

PASSOVER REPRESENTS THE CRUCIFIXION
Each year at Passover, a lamb is slain representing the sin of Israel and ultimately the fall of Adam and Eve. Recognizing the only difference between us and our abusers is the fact that we recognize we've sinned and we've recognized that sin results in death. Israel recognized their offense in Adam, and knew death was sin's curse. Yet when Death came, he passed over their dwelling places, seeing blood on their doorposts as a sign that sin's price has already been paid there. On passover, we are reminded of the nature of sin, its origin in the garden, its rendering in Egypt and ultimate crucifixion in Christ (2 Cor. 5:21).

"Now the Lord said to Moses and Aaron in the land of Egypt, 2 "This month shall be the beginning of months for you; it is to be the first month of the year to you. 3 Speak to all the congregation of Israel, saying, 'On the tenth of this month they are each one to take a lamb for themselves, according to their fathers' households, a lamb for each household. 4 Now if the household is too small for a lamb, then he and his neighbor nearest to his house are to take one according to the number of persons in them; according to what each man should eat, you are to divide the lamb. 5 Your lamb shall be an unblemished male a year old; you may take it from the sheep or from the goats. 6 You shall keep it until the fourteenth day of the same month, then the whole assembly of the congregation of Israel is to kill it at twilight. 7 Moreover, they shall take some of the blood and put it on the two doorposts and on the lintel of the houses in which they eat it. 8 They shall eat the flesh that same night, roasted with fire, and they shall eat it with unleavened bread and bitter herbs. 9 Do not eat any of it raw or boiled at all with water, but rather roasted with fire, both its head and its legs along with its entrails. 10 And you shall not leave any of it over until morning, but whatever is left of it until morning, you shall burn with fire. 11 Now you shall eat it in this manner: with your loins girded, your sandals on your feet, and your staff in your hand; and you shall eat it in haste—it is the Lord's Passover. 12 For I will go through the land of Egypt on that night, and will strike down all the firstborn in the land of Egypt, both man and beast; and against all the gods of Egypt I will execute judgments—I am the Lord. 13 The blood shall be a sign for you on the houses where you live; and when I see the blood I will pass over you, and no plague will befall you to destroy you when I strike the land of Egypt." - Exodus 12:1-13

As you can see from the passage above, God gave Israel some instructions that might seem bizarre to a natural minded person. Yet God used their observance of His command to save them and to paint a picture of what He would one day do.

In verse two, what does God do to help the people of Israel initiate a Jewish Calendar?

How many were to participate and at what time were they supposed to kill the lamb (vs.6)?

What will the blood of the Lamb do for the Israelites (vs.13)?

"Therefore when Pilate heard these words, he brought Jesus out, and sat down on the judgment seat at a place called The Pavement, but in Hebrew, Gabbatha. ^{14} Now it was the day of preparation for the Passover; it was about the sixth hour. And he *said to the Jews, "Behold, your King!" ^{15} So they cried out, "Away with *Him*, away with *Him*, crucify Him!" Pilate said to them, "Shall I crucify your King?" The chief priests answered, "We have no king but Caesar." - John 19:13-15

According to the passage above, on what day was Jesus' trial before Pilate and the Jews?

"I have been crucified with Christ; and it is no longer I who live, but Christ lives in me." - Galatians 2:20

What do the previous two passages tell you about who Christ is and what He did with you on the Cross?

In the passages below, please highlight and make note of the corresponding words paralleling the idea of passover with Moses and the passover with Christ:

Jesus is the Lamb:
"Tell the whole community of Israel that each man is to take a lamb ..." - Exodus 12:3

"John saw Jesus coming toward him and said: 'Look, the Lamb of God, who takes away the sin of the world!'" - John 1:29

Without Defect:
"The animals you choose must be year-old males without defect." - Exodus 12:5

"He committed no sin, and no deceit was found in His mouth." - 1 Peter 2:22 and Isaiah 53:9

His Blood as a Sign:
"The blood will be a sign for you on the houses where you are; and when I see the blood, I will pass over you ..." - Exodus 12:13

"We have been justified by His blood." - Romans 5:9

"In Him we have redemption through His blood." - Ephesians 1:7

Our Death He died:
[8] Now if we have died with Christ, we believe that we shall also live with Him, [9] knowing that Christ, having been raised from the dead, is never to die again; death no longer is master over Him. [10] For the

death that He died, He died to sin once for all; but the life that He lives, He lives to God. [11] Even so consider yourselves to be dead to sin, but alive to God in Christ Jesus.

We are Free from Slavery:
"On that very day the Lord brought the Israelites out of Egypt." - Exodus 12:51

"Commemorate this day, the day you came out of Egypt, out of the land of slavery, because the Lord brought you out of it with a mighty hand. Eat nothing containing yeast." - Exodus 13:3

"... He too shared in their humanity so that by His death He might destroy him who holds the power of death – that is, the devil – and free those who all their lives were held in slavery by their fear of death." - Hebrews 2:14-15

"We were in slavery under the basic principles of the world." - Galatians 4:3

PASSOVER IS ABOUT RELEASING DEBTS!
    Mankind had become slaves (indebted) to sin and death. Jesus came to pay that debt and cleanse us of a guilty conscience. The cross is where all debts were paid once and for all. Passover is all about receiving and giving forgiveness. Forgiveness is about releasing all and any perceived debt.

    Are there any sins committed against you that need to be passed over? Do you forgive debts or do you demand people pay you what they owe you? How often do you give to those who have not earned your generosity? This is what passover is all about-sowing before you reap.

"He made Him who knew no sin to be sin on our behalf, so that we might become the righteousness of God in Him." - 2 corinthians 5:21

FEAST OF UNLEAVENED BREAD / BURIAL

UNLEAVENED BREAD AND THE GARDEN OF EDEN

The feast of unleavened bread has its roots in the garden of eden and bread is a constant theme and symbol throughout the scriptures. In the garden of Eden after Adam fell from grace, God's came to him with correction and said, "by the sweat of your brow you shall eat of this land." So man began tilling the ground to try and grow grain for bread. Did you get that? The curse that came as a result of disobedience was about having to provide our own bread! God later sustained Israel in the wilderness by sending His mana from heaven. In the temple, the priests were called to bring the "bread of the presence" and set it on the table of showbread.

JESUS IS OUR UNLEAVENED BREAD!

In the New Testament, we see Jesus revealed as the fresh mana from heaven. He saves and sustains us in our deserts. He redeems us from the curse of the garden. In Him, the land produces fruit again. He is the seed that goes into the earth, the grave, that produces many fold what was planted. Bread represents God's presence as the source of our sustenance, energy, life and provision. The bread of His presence is the true mana from heaven, His presence is to be consumed as bread on a daily basis. Understanding the biblical symbology and history of bread is important as a backdrop for understanding the true meaning of the feast of unleavened bread.

THE FEAST OF UNLEAVENED BREAD

Part of God's instruction for the Days of Unleavened Bread is to get all leaven out of Israel (Exodus:12:15-16). In the scriptures, leaven represents sin. Especially the sin of religious pride - like leaven, knowledge puffs up, but the scriptures contrast leaven to love in that love builds up (1 Corinthians 8:1). Just as the Passover was fulfilled in the crucifixion of Christ, Unleavened Bread is fulfilled in the burial of Christ.

UNLEAVENED BREAD REPRESENTS BURIAL OF SIN

It is important that our old nature was not only crucified with Christ, but it was buried with Him as well. No one wants a dead carcass following them around! Dead things need to be buried! Crosses were not meant to be carried for long. The only time you can carry a cross is the time before you are crucified on it. Some are still carrying around their old carcasses. In the new testament, baptism is an act through which we choose to unite ourselves nto the finished work of His Cross and consign our old sinful nature into the custody of His grave.

"What shall we say then? Are we to continue in sin so that grace may increase? ² May it never be! How shall we who died to sin still live in it? ³ Or do you not know that all of us who have been baptized into Christ Jesus have been baptized into His death? ⁴ Therefore we have been buried with Him through baptism into death, so that as Christ was raised from the dead through the glory of the Father, so we too might walk in newness of life. ⁵ For if we have become united with Him in the likeness of His death,

certainly we shall also be in the likeness of His resurrection, ⁶ knowing this, that our old self was crucified with Him, in order that our body of sin might be done away with, so that we would no longer be slaves to sin; ⁷ for he who has died is freed from sin." - Romans 6:1-7

WHAT ARE YOU HUNGRY FOR?
"Keep the feast, not with old leaven, nor with the leaven of malice and wickedness (lingering sinful attitudes), but with the unleavened bread of sincerity and truth" — 1 Corinthians 5:8 a clear reference to the Feast of Unleavened Bread." - (emphasis added)

Paul recognized that the unleavened bread of this Feast is symbolic of sincerity and truth, which should be hallmarks of the life of every Christian. He also understood that leaven during this time symbolized sin, and this Feast pictures our need to make every effort to eliminate it completely from our lives.

The truly great story about the days of unleavened bread is the story of the resurrected Christ living His life through those of us who have received His Spirit! This empowers us to overcome sin in a way that previously was simply not possible.

The Feast of Unleavened Bread is a festival celebrating the replacement of an appetite for sin with an appetite for righteousness. But the only real way to get the bread of sin out of our bellies is to put the bread of Jesus Christ *into* our bellies! We are promised that we can truly put sin out of our lives because Jesus Christ has entered within us as the communion bread of life! (Galatians:2:20)

"Clean out the old leaven so that you may be a new lump, just as you are in fact unleavened. For Christ our Passover also has been sacrificed." - 1 Corinthians 5:7

Just as the dough must enter the fire before it becomes bread, so too, Christ entered the fires of hell (Hades - The Grave) for us. He endured the fires of hell for us even though He was without the leaven of sin! Our knowledge has the power to puff us up, but only His love could resurrect us.

In the Feast of Passover, Christ crucified your sin nature (2 Cor. 5:21). In the Feast of Unleavened Bread, Christ buried your sin nature (Col 2:12). Your old BC nature has not only died, its residue and carcass has been buried! It has been separated as far from you as the east is from the west! You are free!

"Having been buried with Him in baptism, in which you were also raised up with Him through faith in the working of God, who raised Him from the dead." - Colossians 2:12

Unleavened bread is about the burial of things that have died. Is there anything that needs to be buried in your life?

Is there any leaven in your life that needs to be replaced with the righteousness of Christ?

FEAST OF FIRST FRUITS / RESURRECTION

FIRST FRUITS WITH ADAM AND EVE

First Fruits is a Holy Day aimed at blessing God for the Spring time crops. The idea of giving God the first fruits goes all the way back to Adam and Eve when Adam and Eve took the fruit from the tree of the knowledge of good and evil. The theme continued when Adam and Eve's children, Cain and Able, one day each brought God an offering. Able brought God a "first fruits" offering, but Cain just brought God an offering. The difference being that Cain, like his parents, served his carnal appetite by eating first before giving to God, while Able gave God the "first fruits," and only after did he eat, thus demonstrating his mastery over the serpent's temptations. God is not some ego-crazed deity who demands sacrifices from us for no reason. He was hoping His children would learn a lesson where their parents failed - practicing spiritual dominion over their own fleshly appetites and over the devil's temptations. Able passed the test God wanted them both to pass by bringing God his "first fruits offering"

FIRST FRUITS AND THE RULE OF MAN OVER EARTH

As time went on, the feast of first fruits was established as a celebration of the harvest and the first fruits of God's provision. Each year the Israelites were dependent on God to provide rain and sun for their crops to grow. Each year it was a nail-biting affair, waiting to see how the crops would turn out. When the first fruits of the Spring harvest finally arrived, there was an obvious sense of relief that would come as their provision (food) for the year had begun to show! As the formation of Israel's national sovereignty was dawning under Moses' leadership, one of the pillars of that independence was the establishment of these seven feasts. I would guess that as Moses was setting up the feast of first fruits for the nation, he was thinking of the garden of

Eden and how this feast represented Israel's control over their own fleshly appetites (like Able) as well as their dominion over the serpent's temptations where their ancestors (Adam and Eve) had failed.

During the feast of first fruits Israel would give the first portion of crops to God as a sacrifice, which was a prophetic act honoring God as the Lord of the Harvest, and recognizing Him as the ultimate source of all life and provision.

RESURRECTION FULFILLS FIRST FRUITS

In the New Testament, Christ is revealed as the fulfillment of this feast; He is the first fruits of mankind, He was the first to show what this new Spirit-Filled, resurrected race would look like, and He was the first to conquer death. Resurrection is exactly what the New Testament links to First Fruits. Just as in the feast of First Fruits, the first harvest of a crop was burnt and the smoke and flavor of it rose to heaven, so Jesus was the first to rise to heaven.

"For I delivered to you as of first importance what I also received, that Christ died for our sins according to the Scriptures, [4] and that He was buried, and that He was raised on the third day according to the Scriptures... [17] and if Christ has not been raised, your faith is worthless; you are still in your sins. [18] Then those also who have fallen asleep in Christ have perished. [19] If we have hoped in Christ in this life only, we are of all men most to be pitied. [20] But now Christ has been raised from the dead, the first fruits of those who are asleep. [21] For since by a man came death, by a man also came the resurrection of the dead. [22] For as in Adam all die, so also in Christ all will be made alive. [23] But each in his own order: Christ the first fruits, after that those who are

Christ's at His coming, ^{24} then comes the end, when He hands over the kingdom to the God and Father, when He has abolished all rule and all authority and power. ^{25} For He must reign until He has put all His enemies under His feet. ^{26} The last enemy that will be abolished is death." - 1 Corinthians 15:3-4, 20-26

What does the passage above tell you about the order of the resurrection?

"If Christ had not been raised than you are still in your sin..." According to verse 17 of the passage above, does your being "in sin" depend on your own actions, or the actions of another?

According to the same passage (vs. 17), what event ultimately removed you completely from your sin nature?

    It is interesting to notice that it was the resurrection of Christ that completed the separation between us and sin. When our sin was crucified with Christ it was still present, even though it died. When our sin was buried with Christ it could still be present and waiting for us in death. But when Christ raised us from the dead, He left our old nature behind and gave us a new one. Its called regeneration, or being born again. We are no longer slaves to sin.

In your estimation, what percentage of your life is spent serving your carnal appetites verses your spiritual appetites? What percentage are you hungrier for God than you are for food?

FEAST OF PENTECOST / NATIONAL SOVEREIGNTY:

PASSOVER LINKED FROM ADAM AND EVE

"Pentecost" is literally the Greek word for "Fifty." Fifty days after Passover is when Pentecost is celebrated. It is also called the "Feast of Weeks" as it begins 7 weeks (seven sevens - or 49 days) from Pentecost. In the Seven days of the Creation account in Genesis, we find God resting on the sabbath or seventh day after completing all His work. The book of Hebrews reveals God has been in that sabbath state of rest from that day until now. His presence is rest. If we return to His presence, we return to the realm of His rest.

As pentecost is the seventh seven from the day of passover, it represents entering the complete finished work of Christ, the complete presence of God, and the complete union with His Spirit, resulting in the ultimate rest and return to Eden, the reverse of the curse of the land! Rest is the Gospel. Just as the human race was cursed in the Garden, the curse being, "by the sweat of your brow you will eat of this land." Now, Pentecost, having followed first fruits of God's provision, celebrates God's deliverance from the curse of endless labors and the restoration of union with God and His presence. Pentecost, (the Feast of Weeks) is all about entering the presence of God and because God is at rest, His presence means rest. Its about God delivering us out of the hands of our enemies, about God making us One nation, about God's forgiveness, provision and favor!!!

Hebrews chapter 4 says it like this:
"Now, God has offered us the promise that we may receive that rest he spoke about. Let us take care, then, that none of you will be found to have failed to receive that promised rest. [2] For we have heard

the Good News, (about Gods rest) just as they did. They heard the message, but it did them no good, because when they heard it, they did not accept it with faith. ³ We who believe, then, do receive that rest which God promised. It is just as he said, "I was angry and made a solemn promise: 'They will never enter the land where I would have given them rest!'" He said this even though his work had been finished from the time he created the world. ⁴ For somewhere in the Scriptures this is said about the seventh day: "God rested on the seventh day from all his work." ⁵ This same matter is spoken of again: "They will never enter that land where I would have given them rest." ⁶ Those who first heard the Good News (of entering His rest) did not receive that rest, because they did not believe. There are, then, others who are allowed to receive it. ⁷ This is shown by the fact that God sets another day, which is called "Today." Many years later he spoke of it through David in the scripture already quoted: "If you hear God's voice today, do not be stubborn." ⁸ If Joshua had given the people the rest that God had promised, God would not have spoken later about another day. ⁹ As it is, however, there still remains for God's people a rest like God's resting on the seventh day. ¹⁰ For those who receive that rest which God promised will rest from their own work, just as God rested from his. ¹¹ Let us, then, do our best to receive that rest, so that no one of us will fail as they did because of their lack of faith. - Hebrews 4:1-11 (GNT)

ISRAEL'S NATIONAL BIRTHDAY (MOSES)

Earlier in this chapter we saw that Passover was declared a national holiday to commemorate the day Israel was freed from Egypt to pursue the promise God gave them to become their own nation and possess their own land. Now, fifty days later, having passed through the red sea, still wondering in the wilderness, they come to Mount Sinai and Moses went up on the mountain and had an encounter with God. During this encounter, God gave him the two tablets with the ten commandments and the law. This supernatural exchange emboldened Israel and the material tablets of stone become the supernatural sign from God that they were now a sovereign nation. Could you imagine having two tablets that contained God's own handwriting? Fear and excitement filled the camp and even many other nations who heard of it. The day of Pentecost became Israel's independence day and their National Birthday.

PENTECOST TIES ISRAEL'S IDENTITY TO THE LAW OF MOSES

We can see from this how tied together Israel's national identity was with their law. The law wasn't just something they needed to bring order to their nation, their law was the nation. It defined them as a nation, distinguished them, and set them apart from all other nations. Israel was founded upon the law. The law is Israel. Israel is the law... When the law was born, Israel was born. This explains why the observant Jews are so tied to the Torah. Torah is everything to them!

HOLY SPIRIT FULFILLED PENTECOST

The fulfillment of this day came 50 days after the Passover on which Jesus was crucified, Right on the day of pentecost. Just as the law came down from heaven, the Holy Spirit came down from heaven on this day to be unto us the fulfillment of the law, that it would no longer be an external thing, but an internal one.

The Spirit came on pentecost to initiate the Churches birthday. The Spirit came on this day because God wanted to restore us to a similar state as we had in the garden. We went from knowing God, to knowing good and evil, to knowing God's law, and in the Sprit, to truly knowing God again!

But now we have been released from the Law, having died to that by which we were bound, so that we serve in newness of the Spirit and not in oldness of the letter. - Romans 7:6

3 For what the Law could not do, weak as it was through the flesh, God did: sending His own Son in the likeness of sinful flesh and as an offering for sin, He condemned sin in the flesh, 4 so that the requirement of the Law might be fulfilled in us, who do not walk according to the flesh but according to the Spirit. 5 For those who are according to the flesh set their minds on the things of the flesh, but those who are according to the Spirit, the things of the Spirit. - Romans 8:3-5

But if you are led by the Spirit, you are not under the Law. - Galatians 5:18

3 being manifested that you are a letter of Christ, cared for by us, written not with ink but with the Spirit of the living God, not on tablets of stone but on tablets of human hearts. 4 Such confidence we have through Christ toward God. 5 Not that we are adequate in ourselves to consider anything as coming from ourselves, but our adequacy is from God, 6 who also made us adequate as servants of a new covenant, not of the letter but of the Spirit; for the letter kills, but the Spirit gives life. 7 But if the ministry of death, in letters engraved on stones, came with glory, so that the sons of Israel could not look intently at the face of Moses because of the glory of his face, fading as it was, ⁸ how will the ministry of the Spirit fail to be even more with glory? ⁹ For if the ministry of condemnation has glory, much more does the ministry of righteousness abound in glory. ¹⁰ For indeed what had glory, in this case has no glory because of the glory that surpasses it. ¹¹ For if that which fades away was with glory, much more that which remains is in glory. ¹² Therefore having such a hope, we use great boldness in our speech, ¹³ and are not like Moses, who used to put a veil over his face so that the sons of Israel would not look intently at the end of what was fading away. ¹⁴ But their minds were hardened; for until this very day at the reading of the old covenant the same veil remains unlifted, because it is removed in Christ. ¹⁵ But to this day whenever Moses is read, a veil lies over their heart; ¹⁶ but whenever a person turns to the Lord, the veil is taken away. ¹⁷ Now the Lord is the Spirit, and where the Spirit of the Lord is, there is liberty. ¹⁸ But we all, with unveiled face, beholding as in a mirror the glory of the Lord, are being transformed into the same image from glory to glory, just as from the Lord, the Spirit. - 2 Corinthians 3:3-18*

"⁷ For if that first covenant had been faultless, there would have been no occasion sought for a second. ⁸ For finding fault with them, He says, "Behold, days are coming, says the Lord, When I will effect a new covenant With the house of Israel and with the house of Judah; ⁹ Not like the covenant which I made with their fathers on the day when I took them by the hand To lead them out of the land of Egypt; For they did not continue in My covenant, And I did not care for them, says the Lord. ¹⁰ "For this is the covenant that I will make with the house of Israel After those days, says the Lord: I will put My *laws into their minds, And I will write them on their hearts. And I will be their God, And they shall be My people. ^{11} "And they shall not teach everyone his fellow citizen, And everyone his brother, saying, 'Know the Lord,' For all will know Me, From the least to the greatest of them. ^{12} "For I will be merciful to their iniquities, And I will remember their sins no more." ^{13} When He said, "A new covenant," He has made the first obsolete. But whatever is becoming obsolete and growing old is ready to disappear."* - Hebrews 8:7-13

In your estimation, how much do you live by the spirit verses by the law?

THE FALL FEASTS: TRUMPETS, ATONEMENT AND TABERNACLES

The first four of the seven feasts occur during the springtime (Passover, Unleavened Bread, First Fruits, and Weeks or Pentecost), and they all have already been clearly fulfilled in the New Testament. The final three holidays (Trumpets, the Day of Atonement, and Tabernacles) occur during the fall and many Bible scholars believe these fall feasts have not yet been fulfilled. Since these feasts were mentioned in an order, many believe they will be fulfilled in the same order. Just as the four spring feasts were clearly and publicly fulfilled literally and right on the actual feast day in connection with Christ's first coming, these three fall feasts, will likewise be fulfilled literally in connection to the Lord's second coming.

We will now look at these feasts in more depth.

FEAST OF TRUMPETS (ROSH HASHANAH) / REPENTANCE

THE HEAD OF THE YEAR

Jewish tradition states that the universe was created by the LORD on Rosh Hashanah (meaning "the head of the year"). Later, The Mishnah *(Sanhedrin 38b) clarifies the dates by saying that God created the Universe on Elul 25, but that He created Adam six days later on Tishri 1, (Rosh Hashanah).* Either way, Yom Kippur (Feast of Atonement) represents our universal birthday as mankind.

During Talmudic times, Rosh Hashanah, which means, "the head of the year" also became known as *Yom Teru'ah* or the "Feast of Trumpets." In traditional Judaism, the Feast of Trumpets is celebrated as Jewish New Years Day. The holiday is observed on the first two days of the Hebrew month of Tishri (i.e., the seventh "new moon" of the year), which usually falls in September or October, and marks the beginning of a ten-day period of prayer, self-examination and repentance, which culminates on the Day of Atonement (Yom Kippur). These ten days are referred to as the "Days of Awe," or the High Holy Days.

A DAY OF REMEMBRANCE THROUGH TRUMPETS

In Leviticus 23:24, Rosh Hashanah is also called by yet another name, the "Day of Remembrance," which is a reference to the commandment to remember to blow the shofar to proclaim God as King of the Universe. The blast of the shofar is meant to jolt us from our sleep. We are to *remember* who we really are by remembering who the LORD really is.

Again, this day has its roots in the Garden of Eden. As Adam and Eve turned from the Lord, this day is a trumpet blast to remind those of us who have done the same to turn back and for those of us who have not, to remain.

TRUMPETS LINKED TO THE RETURN OF CHRIST

Ancient Israel understood the use of trumpets as a way of announcing special, very important messages (Numbers:10:1-10). In the New Testament, Jesus reveals that before His return to the earth, there will be the blowing of seven trumpets, announcing progressive stages of the downfall and overthrow of this world's kingdoms, ending with the return of Christ to take possession of the earth. Christ's return is announced by the seventh and final trumpet.

"When the Lamb broke the seventh seal, there was silence in heaven for about half an hour. ² And I saw the seven angels who stand before God, and seven trumpets were given to them." - Revelation 8:2

"Then the seventh angel sounded; and there were loud voices in heaven, saying, 'The kingdom of the world has become the kingdom of our Lord and of His Christ; and He will reign forever and ever.'" - Revelation 11:15

This day also pictures the time when faithful Christians will be resurrected to eternal life at the time of the seventh trumpet to reign with Jesus Christ for 1,000 years (Revelation:20:4-6

"In a moment, in the twinkling of an eye, at the last trumpet; for the trumpet will sound, and the dead will be raised imperishable, and we will be changed." - 1 Corinthians 15:52

"For the Lord Himself will descend from heaven with a shout, with the voice of the archangel and with the trumpet of God, and the dead in Christ will rise first." - 1 Thessalonians 4:16

"Then I saw thrones, and they sat on them, and judgment was given to them. And I saw the souls of those who had been beheaded because of their testimony of Jesus and because of the word of God, and those who had not worshiped the beast or his image, and had not received the mark on their forehead and on their hand; and they came to life and reigned with Christ for a thousand years. ⁵ The rest of the dead did not come to life until the thousand years were completed. This is the first resurrection. ⁶ Blessed and holy is the one who has a part in the first resurrection; over these the second death has no power, but they will be priests of God and of Christ and will reign with Him for a thousand years." - Revelation:20:4-6

TRUMPETS CALL TO REPENT

According to the Talmud the Book of Life is opened every year on Rosh Hashanah, the feast of trumpets. The same source says the book of Life's analog for the wicked, the Book of the Dead is also opened on that day. Both books are kept open for ten days until on the tenth day (the day of atonement) when all the fates of each person are sealed for the next year into the books and they are sealed up once again.

Trumpets announce the event of fates being sealed and books being closed. According to Jewish tradition, these "ten days of awe" are ten days of opportunity to make restitution for any wrong done in the previous year. The ten days of trumpets announce the judgement, correction and opinion of God falling upon mankind, like light upon darkness. This feast offers us ten days to repent and change our thinking before resurrection day in order that our fates might be sealed in the book of life.

As creation was manifest by the utterance of God's word, so too the sons of God are manifest as they hear God's word. *Like the blast of a trumpet, the gospel calls us to repentance and reconciliation. Repentance not just from dead works, but toward reconciliation with God. This is a time to evangelize and call sinners and saints alike to repentance and reconciliation with God.*

How does this Holy Day speak to your life? Every year, it offers an opportunity for a new beginning, it is the dawning of regeneration. It is the birth time of all creation and an opportunity for a rebirth for you. In what ways do you need to be reborn? What things need to be judged and repented for in your life? What things can't survive in God's presence? Its time to let go of those things and fully embrace God.

The remaining fall feast days describe steps in the establishment of the prophesied Kingdom of God on earth and judgments of humanity after Christ's return. The Feast of Trumpets is followed by the Day of Atonement.

FEAST OF ATONEMENT / RECONCILIATION:

THE BOOK OF LIFE AND THE BOOK OF DEATH

As stated in the previous section, according to Jewish tradition, on Rosh Hashanah, (Tishri 1) the destiny of the righteous are written in the Book of

Life, and the destiny of the wicked are written in the Book of Death. However, most people's names will not be inscribed in *either* book until the tenth day -- *until Yom Kippur, the day of atonement* (Tishri 10). Thus giving each person time to repent before sealing their fate. This is why it is called the Ten Days of Repentance. On Yom Kippur, the last trumpet will sound and everyone's name will be sealed in one of the books.

Here is a prophetic psalm of David, as he is foretelling the death of Messiah:

"For they have persecuted him whom You Yourself have smitten, And they tell of the pain of those whom You have wounded. ^{27} Add iniquity to their iniquity, And may they not come into Your righteousness. ^{28} May they be blotted out of the book of life And may they not be recorded with the righteous." - Psalm 69:26-28

David is agonizing about the people's rejection of the Messiah, but notice that he sees the persecutor's names as having already been in the book of life. He is asking God to blot them out so they not be counted among the righteous! Its as if every year, we are repenting from anything that might get our names blotted out, not to get them written in.

ATONEMENT MEANS RECONCILIATION!
In most of the more popular Bible translations, the Greek word for "atonement," which is "Katallaga," is translated "reconciliation." It means "at-one-ment," or becoming ONE with God. The New Testament is filled with passages using the word reconciliation, and therefore invoking the imagery of this feast.

"For if while we were enemies we were reconciled (atoned) to God through the death of His Son, much more, having been reconciled (atoned), we shall be saved by His life. And not only so, but we also joy in God through our Lord Jesus Christ, by whom we have now received the atonement. - Romans 5:10-11 (NASB, KJV mixed)

"Therefore from now on we recognize no one according to the flesh; even though we have known Christ according to the flesh, yet now we know Him in this way no longer. [17] Therefore if anyone is in Christ, he is a new creature; the old things passed away; behold, new things have come. [18] Now all these things are from God, who reconciled (atoned) us to Himself through Christ and gave us the ministry of reconciliation (atoning), [19] namely, that God was in Christ reconciling (atoning) the world to Himself, not counting their trespasses against them, and He has committed to us the word of reconciliation (atonement). [20] Therefore, we are ambassadors for Christ, as though God were making an appeal through us; we beg you on behalf of Christ, be reconciled (atoned) to God. [21] He made Him who knew no sin to be sin on our behalf, so that we might become the righteousness of God in Him." - 2 Corinthians 5:16-21

CHRIST MADE ATONEMENT AND WILL ONE DAY COME TO COLLECT IT

Just like all the other feasts, the feast of Atonement was fulfilled by Christ and will ultimately be consummated in His return. Christ reconciled us, so "be ye reconciled" it says. There is still much of creation not acknowledging to that reconciliation.

"We beg you on behalf of Christ, be reconciled to God." - 2 Corinthians 5:20

The day of Atonement is the tenth and last day of the feast of Trumpets. By the time the day of Atonement has come, Israel had been blowing their trumpets for 9 days, the day of Atonement is considered the day the "last trumpet" would sound. As we said in the last section, this day will likely be the day the Bible refers to as judgment day or resurrection day.

"In a moment, in the twinkling of an eye, at the last trumpet; for the trumpet will sound, and the dead will be raised imperishable, and we will be changed." - 1 Corinthians 15:52

"For the Lord Himself will descend from heaven with a shout, with the voice of the archangel and with the trumpet of God, and the dead in Christ will rise first." - 1 Thessalonians 4:16

Therefore having overlooked the times of ignorance. God is now declaring to men that all people everywhere should repent, ^{31} because He has fixed a day in which He will judge the world in righteousness through a Man whom He has appointed, having furnished proof to all men by raising Him from the dead." - Acts 17:30-31

^{10} But you, why do you judge your brother? Or you again, why do you regard your brother with contempt? For we will all stand before the judgment seat of God. ^{11} For it is written, "As I live, says the Lord, every knee shall bow to Me, And every tongue shall give praise to God." - Romans 14:10-11

For we must all appear before the judgment seat of Christ, so that each one may be recompensed for his deeds in the body, according to what he has done, whether good or bad. - 2 Corinthians 5:10

According to the previous two passages, is anyone exempt from the day of reconciliation?

ALL THINGS ATONED FOR TO BE RENDERED
Traditionally to the Jews, the day of atonement is the day of Judgment. As Christians, we know it as resurrection day. The day all things are fully manifested "in Christ."

In the space provide under the passages below, please make note of what is included in the reconciliation of Christ which will ultimately be manifest on the final day of Atonement:

"Through Him to reconcile all things to Himself, having made peace through the blood of His cross; through Him, *I say,* whether things on earth or things in heaven." - *Colossians 1:20*

"With a view to an administration suitable to the fullness of the times, *that is,* the summing up of all things in Christ, things in the heavens and things on the earth. - *Ephesians 1:10*

What do the following passages tell you about this day?

"For when Gentiles who do not have the Law do instinctively the things of the Law, these, not having the Law, are a law to themselves, [15] *in that they show the work of the Law written in their hearts, their*

conscience bearing witness and their thoughts alternately accusing or else defending them, [16] on the day when, according to my gospel, God will judge the secrets of men through Christ Jesus." - Romans 2:14-16

"He who rejects Me and does not receive My sayings, has one who judges him; the word I spoke is what will judge him at the last day." - John 12:48

"Because He has fixed a day in which He will judge the world in righteousness through a Man whom He has appointed, having furnished proof to all men by raising Him from the dead." - Acts 17:31

"In the future there is laid up for me the crown of righteousness, which the Lord, the righteous Judge, will award to me on that day; and not only to me, but also to all who have loved His appearing." - 2 Timothy 4:8

BE YE RECONCILED!
     Just as John the baptist prepared the way of the Lord through a ministry of repentance, so too the feast of trumpets, and repentance should have prepared a way in you for the Lord's arrival. There is a baptism by fire that is to take place on this day of atonement. When you experience your union with Him, you experience a union with fire. Our God is a consuming fire. His fire will burn away all things that can burn. All impurities, all sin, all guilt, all shame! This is His judgment. All that will remain of you is that which was born of Him. Are you ready for His presence?

* Please see note on "The Christian Orthodox view of Judgment" at the end of this chapter.

Is there any portion of your heart or mind, not yet operating in His reconciliation? Are you still feeling condemned and separated? Do you still maintain a guilty conscience? Do you still need the gospel preached to you that it might produce repentance in you?

Consider yourselves dead in Christ! It is time for atonement!

FEAST OF TABERNACLES / COHABITATION: & SHALOM

The Feast of tabernacles is also called "Sukkot" in Hebrew. Five days after the Day of Atonement, the feast of tabernacles begins.

ROOTS IN THE GARDEN
In the garden of Eden, Adam and Eve lived in God's presence. They "tabernacled" with God. When they left God's presence, they removed themselves from His tent. Ever since then, He has been planning out the restoration of our cohabitation.

THE FEAST OF TABERNACLES

Feast of Tabernacles is a week-long fall festival commemorating the 40-year journey of the Israelites in the wilderness. The word *Sukkot* means "booths." To the Israelites the Feast of Tabernacles depicted their forty years of wandering in the wilderness before entering the Promised Land.

"You shall keep the Feast of Sukkot seven days, when you have gathered in the produce... You shall

rejoice in your feast... because the LORD your God will bless you in all your produce and in all the work of your hands, so that you will be altogether joyful."
- *Deuteronomy 16:13-15*

According to the passage above, what are some of the words and ideas that God associates with this feast?

From an agricultural perspective in ancient Israel, Pesach [Passover] corresponded to the planting season, Shavuot [Pentecost] corresponded to the grain harvest, and Sukkot [Tabernacles] corresponded to the fruit harvest. When you planted your crops in spring, you do not yet rejoice because you were uncertain about how the harvest will turn out. And when you harvested your grain at the start of summer, you might have rejoiced that you now had bread in hand, but you would still be uncertain about the success of your fruit crops. Total joy would come after you had harvested all of your crops in the fall, and thereby received sustenance and provision for the coming year from the LORD. For this reason, Sukkot is sometimes referred to as *Chag Ha-asif*, or "the Feast of Ingathering."

In Biblical times, Sukkot was considered the most important of all the holidays, referred to simply as "the Feast" (1 Kings 12:32). It was a time of many sacrifices (Num. 29:12-40) and a time when (on Sabbatical years) the Torah would be read aloud to the people (Deut. 31:10-13). It is one of the three required festivals of the LORD (Exod. 23:14; Deut. 16:16).

The Torah explicitly commands three things regarding the festival of Sukkot:

1. To gather the "four species" (Lev. 23:40)
2. To rejoice before the LORD (Deut. 16:13-14; Lev. 23:40)
3. To live in a sukkah (Lev. 23:42) or tent.

From a spiritual perspective, Sukkot corresponds to the joy of knowing your sins were forgiven (during Atonement or Yom Kippur), and also recalls God's miraculous provision and care after the deliverance from bondage in Egypt. Prophetically, Sukkot anticipates the return of Jesus the Messiah when He will "tabernacle among us" physically and permanently and all the nations will come to Jerusalem to worship Him during the festival (see Zech. 14:16).

JESUS LIKELY BORN ON THE FEAST OF TABERNACLES!
The Bible does not specifically say the date of Jesus' birth. We know it was not during the winter months because the sheep were in the pasture (Luke 2:8). A study of the time of the conception of John the Baptist reveals he was conceived about Sivan 30, the eleventh week.

When Zechariah was ministering in the temple, he received an announcement from God of a coming son. The eighth course of Abia, when Zekharya was ministering, was the week of Sivan 12 to 18 (Killian n.d.). Adding forty weeks for a normal pregnancy reveals that John the Baptist was born on or about Passover (Nisan 14).

We know six months after John's conception, Mary conceived Jesus (Luke 1:26-33). Therefore, Jesus would have been conceived six months later in the month of Kislev. Kislev 25 is Hanukkah (around December 25th). Was the "light of the world" conceived on the festival of lights? Starting at Hanukkah, which begins on Kislev 25 and counting the nine months of Mary's pregnancy, one arrives at the approximate time of the birth of Jesus at the Festival of Tabernacles (the early fall of the year). We can't say for sure if Jesus was born on Tabernacles, but we know He was born around that time. Given how He fulfilled the other feast days on their actual day, it would not be surprising if Tishri 15 was His actual birthday. It is highly likely.

During the Feast of Tabernacles, God required all male Jews to come to Jerusalem. The many pilgrims coming to Jerusalem for the festivals would spill over to the surrounding towns (Bethlehem is about five miles from Jerusalem). Joseph and Mary were unable to find a room at the inn because of the influx of so many pilgrims. They may have been given shelter in a sukkah, which is built during a seven-day period each year accompanying the celebration of the Feast of Tabernacles. Due to the difficulties during travel, it was common for the officials to declare tax time during a temple Feast (Luke 2:1).

We know our Messiah was made manifest into a temporary body when He came to earth. Is it possible He also was put into a temporary dwelling? The fields would have been dotted with sukkoths during this harvest time to temporary shelter animals. The Hebrew word "stable" is called a sukkoth (Gen. 33:17).

And she brought forth her firstborn son, and wrapped him in swaddling clothes, and laid him in a manger; because there was no room for them in the inn (Luke 2:7).

Joseph and Mary took the child and flew to Egypt and remained there until they were told by God that Herod was dead. Joseph and Mary brought the baby Jesus into Jerusalem forty days from His birth for Mary's purification and the child's dedication (according to Torah this had to be done within forty days of the birth of a male child-not doing so is considered a sin).

This indicates that Herod died within the same forty days, because as long as Herod was alive, they could not appear at the Temple. (According to Josephus' calculations, Herod's death occurred during the Autumn in the fourth year before the Common Era 4 b.c.e.).

It is interesting that John the baptist had a ministry preaching "a baptism of repentance" and "preparing the way in the wilderness." And upon Jesus' arrival said, "He must increase, I must decrease." He knew that his season was coming to an end and Jesus' was about to begin.

JESUS IS THE FULFILLMENT OF TABERNACLES AND THE COHABITATION OF GOD AND MAN!

"Behold, the virgin shall be with child and shall bear a Son, and they shall call His name Immanuel," which translated means, "God with us." - Matthew 1:23

"And the Word became flesh, and did tabernacle among us, and we beheld his glory, glory as of an only begotten of a father, full of grace and truth." - John 1:14 (YLT)

Today Sukkot celebrates God's start of the New Year. In light of the work of Jesus as our high priest of the New Covenant, we now have access to the Heavenly Temple of God (Heb. 4:16). We are now members of the greater Temple of His body; we are now part of His great Sukkah!

WE ARE HIS TABERNACLE, HE IS OUR TABERNACLE

"For we know that if our earthly house of this tabernacle were dissolved, we have a building of God, an house not made with hands, eternal in the heavens. 2 For in this we groan, earnestly desiring to be clothed upon with our house which is from heaven: 3 If so be that being clothed we shall not be found naked. 4 For we that are in this tabernacle do groan, being burdened: not for that we would be unclothed, but clothed upon, that mortality might be swallowed up of life." - 2 Corinthains 5:1-4

According to 2 Corinthians 5:1-4, what does Paul describe as the true tabernacle?

"13 And shall receive the reward of unrighteousness, as they that count it pleasure to riot in the day time. Spots they are and blemishes, sporting themselves with their own deceivings while they feast with you; 14 Having eyes full of adultery, and that cannot cease from sin; beguiling unstable souls: an heart they have exercised with covetous practices; cursed children." - 2 Peter 2:13-14

According to 2 Peter 2:13-14 what does Peter describe as the true tabernacle?

As you can see, Peter and Paul referred to our physical bodies as tabernacles, or temporary dwellings.

Matthew Henry states: "It is supposed by many that our blessed Savior was born much about the time of this holiday [Feast of Tabernacles]; then He left his mansions of light above to tabernacle among us (John 1:14), and he dwelt in booths. And the worship of God under the New Testament is prophesied of under the notion of keeping the feast of tabernacles, (Zec.14:16). The gospel of Christ teaches us to dwell in tabernacles, to sit loose to this world, as those that have here no continuing city, but by faith, and hope and holy contempt of present things, to go out to Christ without the camp, Heb. 13:13, 14."

SUMMARY OF THE FULFILLMENT OF ALL THE FEASTS

The first three of the feasts, the Spring feasts, start back to back over the course of three days. These feasts have already had their New Covenant fulfillment. They were fulfilled by Jesus Himself in his death, burial, and resurrection. Jesus fulfilled them right on the set calendar dates of the feasts. He entered Jerusalem 2,000 years ago right on the day appointed in His first coming as Messiah by the prophet Daniel (see Daniel 9). He came into Jerusalem as the Suffering Servant, riding on a donkey. Four days later, just as the passover celebrations were being prepared in Israel, the religious leaders turned their sights on Jesus. Oddly enough, just as the Passover lambs were being killed Jesus also bled and gave His life blood for us on the cross of Calvary. It was no coincidence. Surely He was the Lamb of God who takes away the sins of the world!

So He was crucified on Passover, and just as bread is placed in an oven to bake, Jesus was placed in a tomb that night and laid in the tomb just as the Feast of Unleavened Bread was about to start. Three days later, on Nisan 17, the morning after the feast of First Fruits began, Jesus' tomb was empty. He had risen from the grave. He is the first fruits from among the dead.

After Jesus rose from the dead, He appeared to hundreds of people over the course of 40 days teaching them about the Kingdom of God. On the 40th day, He finally ascended to be with the Father telling His followers to wait in Jerusalem until they had been "clothed with power from on high." Ten days later. on the 50th day after passover, the holy day of Pentecost, the Holy Spirit fell upon 120 people in the upper room and the Church was born!

The Holy Spirit outpouring seen that day was unprecedented and glorious. The revival of Israel spread into the city of Jerusalem and then to Judea, Samaria, and eventually to the utmost parts of the earth. Thus was fulfilled the summer Feast of Pentecost. This epic event happened right on the very day of the Hebrew calendar that saw Moses bring the Law down from Mount Sinai to the children of Israel. The Feast of Pentecost was Israel's birthday. Israel's birthday is also turned out to be the birthday of the Church! - Gal.3:29, Rom.11, Eph.2:12-13, 1Pet. 2:9

In the following centuries, humanity will again be visited by God on these days. The fulfillment of the fall feasts eminently awaits, and who knows how many more feast cycles God will again visit us upon.

In the Feast of Trumpets, God gives us ten days each year to make amends for any foul play and reconcile any breaches in relationship with Him and violations of our union with Christ. On the tenth day, the Day of Atonement, we celebrate His finished work of reconciliation (atonement) in the person of Christ, and enjoy our oneness with Him. Five days later on Tishri 15th, we celebrate Jesus' incarnation, His birth as our Son - the Son of Man, thus sealing the union between God and Man and solidifying God's opinion once and for all that we are indeed His children and He cohabitates our flesh.

WOW! HEY! YAY! HALLELUJAH!!! SELAH.

This next year, join a group in your region who celebrates the feasts of Israel. Bring your understanding of Messiah to the group. It should be eventful!

* NOTE ON THE CHRISTIAN ORTHODOX VIEW OF JUDGMENT:

From www.oca.org (Orthodox Church of America) Volume IV - Spirituality / The Kingdom of Heaven / Heaven and Hell:

"The Kingdom of heaven is already in the midst of those who live the spiritual life. What the spiritual person knows in the Holy Spirit, in Christ and the Church, will come with power and glory for all men to behold at the end of the ages.

The final coming of Christ will be the judgment of all men. His very presence will be the judgment. Now men can live without the love of Christ in their lives. They can exist as if there were no God, no Christ, no Spirit, no Church, no spiritual life. At the end of the ages this will no longer be possible. All men will have to behold the Face of Him who "for us men and our salvation came down from heaven and was incarnate... who was crucified under Pontius Pilate, and suffered and was buried . . . " (Nicene Creed) All will have to look at Him whom they have crucified by their sins: Him "who was dead and is alive again." (Revelation 1-.17-18)

For those who love the Lord, His Presence will be infinite joy, paradise and eternal life. For those who hate the Lord, the same Presence will be infinite torture, hell and eternal death. The reality for both the saved and the damned will be exactly the same when Christ "comes in glory, and all angels with Him," so that "God may be all in all." (I Corinthians 15-28) Those who have God as their "all" within this life will finally have divine fulfillment and life. For those whose "all" is themselves and this world, the "all" of God will be their torture, their punishment and their death. And theirs will be "weeping and gnashing of teeth." (Matthew 8:21, et al.)

The Son of Man will send His angels and they will gather out of His kingdom all causes of sin and all evil doers, and throw them into the furnace of fire; there men will weep and gnash their teeth. Then the righteous will shine like the sun in the Kingdom of their Father. (Matthew 13:41-43)

According to the saints, the "fire" that will consume sinners at the coming of the Kingdom of God is the same "fire" that will shine with splendor in the saints. It is the "fire" of God's love; the "fire" of God Himself who is Love. "For our God is a consuming fire" (Hebrews 12:29) who "dwells in unapproachable light." (I

Timothy 6:16) For those who love God and who love all creation in Him, the "consuming fire" of God will be radiant bliss and unspeakable delight. For those who do not love God, and who do not love at all, this same 66consuming fire" will be the cause of their "weeping" and their "gnashing of teeth."

Thus it is the Church's spiritual teaching that God does not punish man by some material fire or physical torment. God simply reveals Himself in the risen Lord Jesus in such a glorious way that no man can fail to behold His glory. It is the presence of God's splendid glory and love that is the scourge of those who reject its radiant power and light.

... those who find themselves in hell will be chastised by the scourge of love. How cruel and bitter this torment of love will be! For those who understand that they have sinned against love, undergo no greater suffering than those produced by the most fearful tortures. The sorrow which takes hold of the heart, which has sinned against love, is more piercing than any other pain. It is not right to say that the sinners in hell are deprived of the love of God... But love acts in two ways, as suffering of the reproved, and as joy in the blessed! (St. Isaac of Syria, Mystic Treatises)

This teaching is found in many spiritual writers and saints: St. Maximus the Confessor, the novelist Fyodor Dostoevsky. At the end of the ages God's glorious love is revealed for all to behold in the Face of Christ. Man's eternal destiny - heaven or hell, salvation or damnation - depends solely on his response to this love."

7
HE SPEAKS THROUGH HIS HOUSE

GOD'S DWELLING PLACE

The place one lives tells you a lot about their nature, values and interests. From the Nation they live within, to the people they live among, to the house they live in, to the possessions and decorations contained in that house, one's home tells you a lot about them. In the same way, although He has changed locations a couple of times, God has put His home on display for the world to see.

The beauty of the whole Bible and the one great thought revealed through and through is the person and work of Jesus Christ. He is the house of God. He is the key to Scripture. He is the one central theme of the Bible. Know Christ, understand God's thoughts about Him, and you'll understand the Bible.

The types and shadows we find in all the references in the scriptures about His dwelling place are in fact, a set of pictures given directly from the mind of God. By these pictures He would teach us infinite and eternal truth. If we have seen the One who casts the shadow, then the shadow has all the more meaning. As we study the tabernacle in light of Christ, its types and shadows can now reveal the fullness of their original meaning and their significance in relation to Christ and His Bride.

It can be argued that within the pages of the Scriptures we can find five different but coinciding visions of the dwelling place of God. Each one of these would offer volumes of information but the purpose of this book is only to open the door to the various ways through which God speaks. If you want to go deeper, further personal pursuit is encouraged.

As we study each of the five different but coinciding visions of God's dwelling place, we will discover deeper and deeper truths in the unfolding story of God's house, which ultimately reveals what He thinks of us, His Church and our true power, purpose and identity. These five visions include:

1. Jacob's Tabernacle

2. Moses' Tabernacle

3. David's Tabernacle

4. Christ's Tabernacle

THE HOUSE OF GOD ACCORDING TO JACOB

In Genesis 28:10-17, we find the first time in the bible where the "House of God" is spoken of. This passage reveals a lot about what God's dwelling place looks like.

"[10] Then Jacob departed from Beersheba and went toward Haran. [11] He came to a certain place and spent the night there, because the sun had set; and he took one of the stones of the place and put it under his head, and lay down in that place. [12] He had a dream, and behold, a ladder was set on the earth with its top reaching to heaven; and behold, the angels of God were ascending and descending on it. [13] And behold, the Lord stood above it and said, "I am the Lord, the God of your father Abraham and the God of Isaac; the land on which you lie, I will give it to you and to your descendants. [14] Your descendants will also be like the dust of the earth, and you will spread out to the west and to the east and to the north and to the south; and in you and in your descendants shall all the families of the earth be blessed. [15] Behold, I am with you and will keep you wherever you go, and will bring you back to this land; for I will not leave you until I have done what I have promised you." [16] Then Jacob awoke from his sleep and said, "Surely the Lord is in this place, and I did not know it." [17] He was afraid and said, "How awesome is this place! This is none other than the house of God, and this is the gate of heaven." - Genesis 28:10-17

What does Genesis 28:10-17 say about the angels?

"Bless the Lord, you His angels,Mighty in strength, who perform His word,Obeying the voice of His word![21] Bless the Lord, all you His hosts,You who serve Him, doing His will." - Psalm 103:20-21

What does Psalm 103:20-21 say about what angels do?

So when Jacob saw the Angels ascending and descending he was seeing those who were going out to perform the word of the Lord and those coming back from performing the word of the Lord. The house of God is a place where Heaven meets earth. It is the portal through which the angels travel to and from God's presence on their mission to perform His word.

GOD SPEAKS FROM HIS HOUSE

Another thing we see here is that God speaks loud and clear. The House of God is a place where Gods voice can be heard clearly! This is perhaps the most exciting of the revelations found in this passage. Whoever finds access to God's house, finds access to His voice!

In the passage below, please highlight the portions that teach you about your access to God's house, His favor and His voice:

"It happened that while Jesus was praying in a certain place, after He had finished, one of His disciples said to Him, "Lord, teach us to pray just as John also taught his disciples..." [Here, Jesus goes into the Lord's Prayer...] 5 Then He said to them, "Suppose one of you has a friend, and goes to him at midnight and says to him, 'Friend, lend me three loaves; 6 for a friend of mine has come to me from a journey, and I have nothing to set before him'; 7 and from inside he answers and says, 'Do not bother me; the door has already been shut and my children and I are in bed; I cannot get up and give you anything.' 8 I tell you, even though he will not get up and give him anything because he is his friend, yet because of his persistence he will get up and give him as much as he needs. 9 "So I say to you, ask, and it will be given to you; seek, and you will find; knock, and it will be opened to you. 10 For everyone who asks, receives; and he who seeks, finds; and to him who knocks, it will be opened." - Luke 11:1-10

GOD'S PRESENCE AT HIS HOUSE

In the Genesis passage we read earlier about Jacob we read, "16 Then Jacob awoke from his sleep and said, "Surely the Lord is in this place, and I did not know it" (Genesis 28:16). This is perhaps the greatest challenge to the Church throughout history. God is present, but we might not realize it. If we only believed in God's actual living presence with us on a moment by moment basis! How that would change things!

This brings up an interesting principal. God can be completely present without us being aware of it. The truth is, He is omnipresent and He is always totally 100% present. The only thing is that all too often we are not aware of His being so present. I wonder how many things we have missed out on because we were not aware that God was truly present at that time or place. The Gospel message Jesus Himself taught His disciples to preach was, "The kingdom of God is at hand" (Matthew 10:7). Another way to put that is, "God is here!"

"⁷And as you go, preach, saying, 'The kingdom of heaven is at hand.' ⁸ Heal the sick, raise the dead, cleanse the lepers, cast out demons. Freely you received, freely give." - Matthew 10:7-8

JACOB'S CONCLUSION

The Gospel is about God's presence. God's presence is about His house. We are His house! So we can conclude the following things about God's dwelling place from Jacob's Vision:

* The House of God is the place from which angels travel to and from performing God's command.
* The House of God is the place through which God's voice can be heard.
* The House of God is the place God comes and goes from.
* We are the place of His presence whether we know it or not.
* The House of God is a place of rest.

THE TABERNACLE ACCORDING TO MOSES

Now that we understand the house of God as it was originally revealed to Jacob, lets look at how God's dwelling place was revealed to Moses.

"Then He said to Moses, 'Come up to the Lord, you and Aaron, Nadab and Abihu and seventy of the elders of Israel, and you shall worship at a distance. ² Moses alone, however, shall come near to the Lord, but they shall not come near, nor shall the people come up with him...' ⁹ Then Moses went up with Aaron, Nadab and Abihu, and seventy of the elders of Israel, ¹⁰ and they saw the God of Israel; and under His feet there appeared to be a pavement of sapphire, as clear as the sky itself. ¹¹ Yet He did not stretch out His hand against the nobles of the sons of Israel; and they saw God, and they ate and drank.¹² Now the Lord said to Moses, "Come up to Me on the mountain and remain there, and I will give you the stone tablets with the law and the commandment which I have written for their instruction." ...¹⁵ Then Moses went up to the mountain, and the cloud covered the mountain. ¹⁶ The glory of the Lord rested on Mount Sinai, and the cloud covered it for six days; and on the seventh day He called to Moses from the midst of the cloud. ¹⁷ And to the eyes of the sons of Israel the appearance of the glory of the Lord was like a consuming fire on the mountain top. ¹⁸ Moses entered the midst of the cloud as he went up to the mountain; and Moses was on the mountain forty days and forty nights." - Exodus 24:1-18

We see here that God took Moses up on the mountain and revealed Himself to Moses there. The following chapters of Exodus tell us that what Moses saw on the mountain in the Person of God was more than just eyes or face or body! He saw something that God later told Moses to use as a pattern to build a tent. And it wasn't just any tent. He says the following:

"According to all that I am going to show you, as the pattern of the tabernacle and the pattern of all its furniture, just so you shall construct it." - Exodus 25:9 ... "See that you make them after the pattern for them, which was shown to you on the mountain." - Exodus 25:40

The book of Deuteronomy reveals further details into what Moses saw:

"Now this was the workmanship of the lampstand, hammered work of gold; from its base to its flowers it was hammered work; according to the pattern which the Lord had shown Moses, so he made the lampstand." - Numbers 8:4

The New Testament also remembers this event:

"Our fathers had the tabernacle of testimony in the wilderness, just as He who spoke to Moses directed him to make it according to the pattern which he had seen." - Acts 7:44

There are chapters and chapters of detailed description about what Moses built based on the pattern He saw during his encounter with God. The thing Moses built, based on the pattern he saw, was a tabernacle, a crazy-amazing tent, with many symbolic instruments which all speak as parables, pictures and clues into our corporate and personal identity in Messiah. The tabernacle and its instruments were called the "Tabernacle," the "Tent of meeting," or the "Dwelling place" of God.

"Let them construct a sanctuary for Me, that I may dwell among them." Exodus 25:8

According to the passage above, what was the purpose of God in wanting a tabernacle on earth?

Below is an illustration of the tabernacle of Moses.

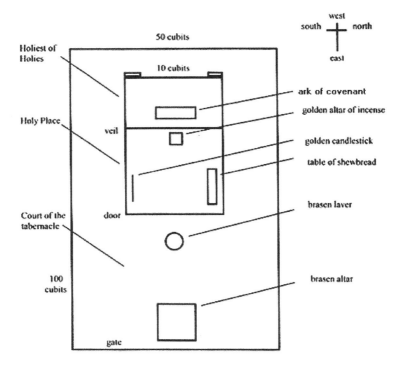

BEZALEL, THE SHADOW OF GOD

God chose a man named Bezalel to be the artisan who created the tabernacle and all its elements. Bezalel is the first person in the Bible said to have been filled with the Spirit of God. Lets see what the Spirit filled him to do:

"Then the Lord said to Moses, 2 "See, I have chosen Bezalel son of Uri, the son of Hur, of the tribe of Judah, 3 and I have filled him with the Spirit of God, with wisdom, with understanding, with knowledge and with all kinds of skills— 4 to make artistic designs for work in gold, silver and bronze, 5 to cut and set stones, to work in wood, and to engage in all kinds of crafts. 6 Moreover, I have appointed Oholiab son of Ahisamak, of the tribe of Dan, to help him. Also I have given ability to all the skilled workers to make everything I have commanded you: 7 the tent of meeting, the ark of the covenant law with the atonement cover on it, and all the other furnishings of the tent— 8 the table and its articles, the pure gold lampstand and all its accessories, the altar of incense, 9 the altar of burnt offering and all its utensils, the basin with its stand— 10 and also the woven garments, both the sacred garments for Aaron the priest and the garments for his sons when they serve as priests, 11 and the anointing oil and fragrant incense for the Holy Place. They are to make them just as I commanded you." - Exodus 31:1-11

  The name "Bezal-el" literally means "Shadow-[of]-God." This is where the later authors of the New Testament get the concept of the law merely being a shadow. In the New Testament we find the idea of the "Shadow of God" referenced a number of times. Comparing the Priesthood of Jesus to that of Moses, the author of Hebrews says, "Now if He were on earth, He would not be a priest at all, since there are those who offer the gifts according to the Law; 5 who <u>serve a copy and shadow</u> of the heavenly things, just as Moses was warned *by God* when he was about to erect the tabernacle; for, "See," He says, "that you make all things according to the pattern which was shown you on the mountain.'" (Hebrews 8:4-5) This is one of a number of examples of the parable that Bezalel presents.

OUTER COURTS REPRESENT THE NATIONS

A "court" is a type of enclosed yard that is open to the sky. It's where we get the word courtyard from. So then the "outer courts" of the tabernacle is the enclosed yard around the tabernacle.

"You shall make the court of the tabernacle. On the south side there shall be hangings for the court of fine twisted linen one hundred cubits long for one side..." - Exodus 27:9

"My soul longed and even yearned for the courts of the Lord; My heart and my flesh sing for joy to the living God. For a day in Your courts is better than a thousand outside. I would rather stand at the threshold of the house of my God Than dwell in the tents of wickedness." - Psalm 84:2,10

"Enter His gates with thanksgiving And His courts with praise. Give thanks to Him, bless His name." - Psalm 100:4

Later, when the temple was erected, its court became the place where trials and judgments were practiced.

"But beware of men, for they will hand you over to the courts and scourge you in their synagogues; - Matthew 10:17

Then the chief priests and the elders of the people were gathered together in the court of the high priest, named Caiaphas; 4 and they plotted together to seize Jesus by stealth and kill Him. - Matthew 26:3-4

It is quite interesting that the outer courts became the place for trials and judgments. Its also interesting that it is man's judgments. Its as if it is saying that passing through the judgments and persecutions of man is a way of purging us and preparing us fully for entering the depths of our union with God.

It's also interesting that the courts are the place all the trading and sacrifices went down. Its saying that Jesus is our entrance point. He is both our sacrifice and our trade.

The outer courts represent the place the Gentiles have been given to access to God, the first heaven, the realm of the nations. Rev. 11:2 says the court outside the temple "has been given to the nations (or Gentiles)." It is interesting that into this "court of nations" has been placed the altar (place of Sacrifice) and the laver (Washing).

The courts teach us about giving people a place who might not feel able to come all the way in at this time. It is a place of cleansing, a place of fellowship and sacrifices. It speaks to our acquaintances. Everyone ought to have an outer court where people can come see and hear their heart. Its the place you give to those who you might not trust completely.

THE GATE OR DOORWAY REPRESENT CHRIST, US

"He was afraid and said, "How awesome is this place! This is none other than the house of God, and this is the gate of heaven." - Genesis 28:17

¹⁴ The hangings for the *one side of the gate shall be* fifteen cubits *with* their three pillars and their three sockets. ¹⁵ And for the other side *shall be* hangings of fifteen cubits *with* their three pillars and their three sockets. ¹⁶ For the gate of the court *there shall be* a screen of twenty cubits, of blue and purple and scarlet *material* and fine twisted linen, the work of a weaver, *with* their four pillars and their four sockets. - Exodus 27:14-16

"Lift up your heads, O gates, And be lifted up, O ancient doors, That the King of glory may come in!" - Psalm 24: 7, 9

"Enter through the narrow gate; for the gate is wide and the way is broad that leads to destruction, and there are many who enter through it. For the gate is small and the way is narrow that leads to life, and there are few who find it." - Matthew 7:13-14

¹¹ *For the bodies of those animals whose blood is brought into the holy place by the high priest as an offering for sin, are burned outside the camp.* ¹² *Therefore Jesus also, that He might sanctify the people through His own blood, suffered outside the gate.* ¹³ *So, let us go out to Him outside the camp, bearing His reproach. Hebrews 13:11-13*

"Truly, truly, I say to you, he who does not enter by the door into the fold of the sheep, but climbs up some other way, he is a thief and a robber. ² But he who enters by the door is a shepherd of the sheep.

³ To him the doorkeeper opens, and the sheep hear his voice, and he calls his own sheep by name and leads them out. ⁴ When he puts forth all his own, he goes ahead of them, and the sheep follow him because they know his voice. ⁵ A stranger they simply will not follow, but will flee from him, because they do not know the voice of strangers." ⁶ This figure of speech Jesus spoke to them, but they did not understand what those things were which He had been saying to them. ⁷ So Jesus said to them again, "Truly, truly, I say to you, I am the door of the sheep. ⁸ All who came before Me are thieves and robbers, but the sheep did not hear them. ⁹ I am the door; if anyone enters through Me, he will be saved, and will go in and out and find pasture. ¹⁰ The thief comes only to steal and kill and destroy; I came that they may have life, and have it abundantly. - John 10:1-10

In these passages, what do you think best represents the gate?

The door or the gate is all about access and permission to go from one place to the next. God is all about giving you freedom to become someone you might not have been at birth. If you were born outside the camp, there is a doorway you can use to come in. It speaks of order. - What good is a doorway if there is not a completed fence? There is a completed fence in heaven and there is only one doorway as the legitimate entrance in.

We can learn from this to make doorways for people to enter into relationship with us in our world in a healthy way. Covenant defines relationship and the doorways of deeper entrance into deeper relationship.

THE BRAZEN ALTAR / SACRIFICE - THE CROSS

[The Bronze Altar] "And you shall make the altar of acacia wood, five cubits long and five cubits wide; the altar shall be square, and its height shall be three cubits." - Exodus 27:1

"Therefore if you are presenting your offering at the altar, and there remember that your brother has something against you, ^{24} leave your offering there before the altar and go; first be reconciled to your brother, and then come and present your offering." - Matthew 5:23-24

The Altar is all about what Christ did for us on the cross. Atonement. Reconciliation. Its all about sacrifices of love. Speaks to us about proper protocol of love. Labor of love, work of faith, perseverance of hope.

THE BRONZE LAVER - WASHING / WORD OF CHRIST

All about washing. In each of us is the ability to wash others through the word of Christ, the Gospel of their identity in Him and His completed view of them. People will wash in your word, in your love.

In the days of Moses, the women didn't have any mirrors as we do today. Instead, they used polished bronze as mirrors to view their image. When Moses took an offering for the Temple to be made, Exodus 35-36 tells us they gave so much that Moses had to ask them to stop giving! One of the things given that day was all the ladies bronze mirrors. These bronze mirrors are what Moses used to melt and mould the bronze laver which was the wash basin that would hold the water for the priests to wash in.

"Moreover, he made the laver of bronze with its base of bronze, from the mirrors of the serving women who served at the doorway of the tent of meeting." - Exodus 38:8

Paul, likely thinking of this imagery, wrote his interpretation of what the laver truly represented to the Corinthian Church. In the space provided under the passage below, please describe what Paul revelation about the mirror:

"But we all, with unveiled face, beholding as in a mirror the glory of the Lord, are being transformed into the same image from glory to glory, just as from the Lord, the Spirit." - 2 Corinthians 3:18

Jesus is the mirror. As we look into Him, we see our true identity. He is our Son, the Son of Man. He reveals our true identity and purpose.

THE HOLY PLACE & THE HOLY OF HOLIES

In the tabernacle of Moses, after you pass through the outer courts you would enter the Holy place. The Holy Place was a rectangular room with three elements inside. On the right was the Table of Showbread, on the left was the Golden Lampstand and in the middle was

Behind the altar of incense on the opposite wall of the entrance to the Holy Place, there was a second doorway that led into the Holy of Holies. The Holy of Holies was a square room with the Ark of the Covenant or "Mercy Seat" resting inside. Inside the

Ark of the Covenant were three objects, the two tables containing the Ten Commandments, Aarons budding staff and mana. The Holy of Holies represented the very presence of God and the priests would regularly encounter Him in tangible and often frightening ways in this room.

Below is a table comparing the elements in both the Holy place and Holy of Holies with the New Testament Equivalent:

Article	Old Covenant Significance	New Testament Revelation
Ark of the Covenant/ Mercy Seat	A symbol of God's law, the Ark was made of wood covered with gold. The Ark was the throne of God where His glory rest on the Mercy Seat (top), a symbol of His mercy. The sacrificed blood was sprinkled on the Ark to cover the sins of the people.	The phrase "Mercy Seat" also means "propitiation." Jesus is the propitiation for us today (Romans 3:25; I John 2:2.) His blood was shed to cleanse our sins. We come to God through Him and offer our spiritual sacrifices (I Peter 2:5,9).
The Inner Veil	The Inner Veil hung between the Holy Place and the Holy of Holies and was passed only once a year by the High Priest on the Day of Atonement (Leviticus 16).	Hebrews 10:19-20 teaches that this Veil represents Christ's body which was given for us on the cross. When He offered up His spirit, the veil in the temple was torn from top to bottom, thus allowing anyone to come at any time into God's presence (Matthew 27:50-51).

Article	Old Covenant Significance	New Testament Revelation
Altar of Incense	Incense was continually burned at this altar that stood before the veil separating the Holy Place from the Holy of Holies. The High Priest was to make atonement on its horns once a year before entering the Holy of Holies.	The Altar of Incense was a symbol of prayer. Christians are to be continually in prayer (Romans 12:12).
Table of Showbread	A symbol of God's providence, the Table held the twelve loaves of bread that were a reminder that the tribes were constantly in the presence of God and that God saw all that they did (Leviticus 24:5-9). The bread also reminded the people that God fed His people.	God provides what we need (Matthew 6:25-34). We as Christians are daily in God's presence. We are to "feed on" God's truth (Matthew 4:4). Jesus is the Bread of Life (John 6:35). For this reason we take communion.
Golden Lampstand	Symbolizing light from God, the intricately patterned Lampstand moulded into almond branches was to give light continually, fueled by clear olive oil (Exodus 27:20) Almond trees - the first of Israel's trees to blossom each year, symbol of the prophetic gift - first ones to know the seasons turnings.	Rev. 1:12-20 indicates local churches are represented by golden lampstands. Jesus is the light of the world (John 8:12). Christians are to be a light to the world, also (Matthew 5:14). filled with the oil (anointing) of Christ, burning with the Fire of the Spirit, prophesying.

When God gave Moses instructions to build the Tabernacle, its design will reflect God's plan creating for Himself a permanent dwelling place in the earth. His dwelling began in the earthly tabernacle, but the final dwelling place or temple for God is in the body of Christ - His spiritual tabernacle. We are the body of Messiah, the temple of God.

"Jesus answered and said unto them, Destroy this temple, and in three days I will raise it up. (20) Then said the Jews, Forty and six years was this temple in building, and wilt thou rear it up in three days? (21) But he spake of the temple of his body." - John 2:19-21(KJV)

"Know ye not that ye are the temple of God, and that the Spirit of God dwelleth in you?" - 1 Corinthians 3:16 (KJV)

"And what agreement hath the temple of God with idols? For ye are the temple of the living God; as God hath said, "I will dwell in them, and walk in them; and I will be their God, and they shall be my people." - 2 Corinthians 6:16 (KJV)

As you can see, Moses' tabernacle design foreshadows the work of God building His final temple in the earth through Christ and through the processes of redemption - salvation, sanctification and glorification. So, the design will be inclusive of God coming to man through Christ, man coming to God and the final perfection of the body of Christ - His temple.

NOTE: It is interesting that when John sees heaven in the book of Revelation, he sees virtually the same thing as Moses, Just labeled differently. Check out Revelation 21:10-27 to compare their notes!

MOSES' CONCLUSION

So we can conclude the following things about God's dwelling place from Moses' Vision:

* The House of God has Outer Courts - a place for foreigners and strangers to come make sacrifices and be cleansed (Outer Courts, Altar & Laver)
* The House of God has One defined doorway through which people can enter (Door)
* Those who enter the House of God will experience fellowship and friendship with God. (Bread)
* Those who enter the House of God will experience illumination and revelation (light)
* Those who enter the House of God will be heard by God (Incense)
* Those who enter the House of God will have access to His Word, His Judgments, His Testimony, and His Mercy. (Mercy Seat)

THE TABERNACLE ACCORDING TO DAVID

Many generations after Moses, when King David came to power, he established what the Bible refers to as "the tabernacle of David," which was yet another foreshadow of the New Covenant Church.

In the book of Acts, we follow the Apostles as they spread the message of Christ throughout much of the Mediterranean region. Halfway through, the book of acts reveals a huge problem. Many Gentiles had begun to receive Christ and become baptized in the Spirit but they had not come in through circumcision or through observing any Old Testament law. The Church, which at that time was almost entirely Jewish, had thought that Gentiles who were impure at birth, had to become circumcised in order to be accepted amongst the Lords elect. It was nothing short of a question about the validity of the entire Old Testament and the Law.

In Acts 15 this issue had finally come to the surface and all the Apostles and major leaders in the Church had gathered to discuss and debate the issue of Gentile conversion and even greater, the role of the Old Testament Law. The conclusion of this debate would decide the fate of Christianity as we know it as it determined how the church understood the Gospel message itself.

"Some men came down from Judea and began teaching the brethren, "Unless you are circumcised according to the custom of Moses, you cannot be saved." [2] And when Paul and Barnabas had great dissension and debate with them, the brethren determined that Paul and Barnabas and some others of them should go up to Jerusalem to the apostles and elders concerning this issue. [3] Therefore, being sent on their way by the church, they were passing through both Phoenicia and Samaria, describing in detail the conversion of the Gentiles, and were bringing great joy to all the brethren. [4] When they arrived at Jerusalem, they were received by the church and the apostles and the elders, and they reported all that God had done with them. [5] But some of the sect of the Pharisees who had believed stood up, saying, "It is necessary to circumcise them and to direct them to observe the Law of Moses." [6] The apostles and the elders came together to look into this matter. [7] After there had been much debate, Peter stood up and said to them, "Brethren, you know that in the early

days God made a choice among you, that by my mouth the Gentiles would hear the word of the gospel and believe. [8] And God, who knows the heart, testified to them giving them the Holy Spirit, just as He also did to us; [9] and He made no distinction between us and them, cleansing their hearts by faith. [10] Now therefore why do you put God to the test by placing upon the neck of the disciples a yoke which neither our fathers nor we have been able to bear? [11] But we believe that we are saved through the grace of the Lord Jesus, in the same way as they also are." [12] All the people kept silent, and they were listening to Barnabas and Paul as they were relating what signs and wonders God had done through them among the Gentiles. [13] After they had stopped speaking, James answered, saying, "Brethren, listen to me. [14] Simeon has related how God first concerned Himself about taking from among the Gentiles a people for His name. [15] With this the words of the Prophets agree, just as it is written, [16] 'After these things I will return, And I will rebuild the tabernacle of David which has fallen, And I will rebuild its ruins, And I will restore it, [17] So that the rest of mankind may seek the Lord, And all the Gentiles who are called by My name,' [18] Says the Lord, who makes these things known from long ago. [19] Therefore it is my judgment that we do not trouble those who are turning to God from among the Gentiles, [20] but that we write to them that they abstain from things contaminated by idols and from fornication and from what is strangled and from blood." (The minimum requirements as spoken of earlier in this book.) - Acts 15:1-20

According to Acts 15:1-2, what was the argument and what was the result?

According to Acts 15:3-5, what were they describing about the Gentiles (vs 3) and what was the believing pharisees response in Jerusalem (vs 5)?

In Acts 15:6-12, what does Peter say about his own calling and about the evidence of God's own approval of the Gentiles regardless of circumcision?

According to Acts 15:13-19, what was James' verdict?

Evidently, the Gentiles were being approved by God and immersed in the Holy Spirit without observing any Jewish law, custom or tradition, buy merely by believing in Jesus! In Acts 15, we see Peter describing this revelation and we see James conclude by pointing back to a prophecy given by Amos in the Old Testament. In Acts 15:16-18, James directly quotes Amos 9:11-12. We see him saying the Tabernacle of David will be rebuilt *SO THAT the rest of mankind may seek the Lord, and all the Gentiles will enter the Kingdom!*

The Tabernacle of David is the name given to the tent that King David set up on Mount Zion in Jerusalem to house the Ark of the Covenant. The Ark of the Covenant was originally housed in the Tabernacle of Moses (also called the Tabernacle of the Congregation). In the year 1050 B.C., David brought the Ark to Jerusalem and placed it in a tent. This tent became known as the Tabernacle of David *(2 Samuel 6, 1 Chronicles 13-16)*. The Ark stayed in David's Tabernacle for 40 years until it was moved into the Temple built and dedicated by David's son Solomon in 1010 B.C. *(2 Chronicles 5-7).*

During the 40 years when the ark was without a permanent house, David created what seems to be a new order of priesthood and worship which stood in sharp contrast to the worship of Moses' Tabernacle. David's version of ministry was to become a prophetic picture of the joyful and exuberant worship that would come during the New Covenant and it would be so ecstatic that even the Gentiles would all get drawn into it! Amos, looking back to Davids days, also looked ahead to the New Covenant and basically said, thats what it will be like! This is exactly what James received the revelation of in Acts 15!

FOUR CONTRASTS & CHARACTERISTICS OF THE NEW COVENANT PRIESTHOOD AS SEEN IN THE TABERNACLE OF DAVID:

1. JOYFUL SACRIFICES OF PRAISE INSTEAD OF SOLEMN SACRIFICES OF ANIMALS

In 1 Chronicles 14-16, we see the story of David's tabernacle. He appointed some of the Levites as ministers before the ark of the Lord, even to celebrate and to thank and praise the Lord God of Israel: ...^{8} Oh give thanks to the Lord, call upon His name; Make known His deeds among the peoples. ^{9} Sing to Him, sing praises to Him; Speak of all His wonders. ^{10} Glory in His holy name; Let the heart of those who seek the Lord be glad. ^{11} Seek the Lord and His strength; Seek His face continually." - 1 Chronicles 16:4-11

1 Chron. 16:4, 8-11, what was the general feel of priestly service?

"Let us come before His presence with thanksgiving, Let us shout joyfully to Him with psalms." - Psalm 95:2

"Enter His gates with thanksgiving And His courts with praise. Give thanks to Him, bless His name." - Psalm 100:4

What type of worship did David describe in *Psalm 95:2 and 100:4?*

" Through Him then, let us continually offer up a sacrifice of praise to God, that is, the fruit of lips that give thanks to His name." - Hebrews 13:15

"But you are a chosen race, a royal priesthood, a holy nation, a people for God's own possession, so that you may proclaim the excellencies of Him who has called you out of darkness into His marvelous light." - 1 Peter 2:9

According to Hebrews 13:15 and 1 Peter 2:9, *what are the sacrifices of the New covenant priesthood as opposed to the animal sacrifices of the old?*

Instead of solemn sacrifices of animals, the tabernacle of David was to serve with sacrifices of thanks, praise and joy. This was a prophetic priesthood, looking forward in celebration to what the Messiah would accomplish - the forgiveness and redemption of the entire human race!

2. BASED ON FAITH OF ABRAHAM INSTEAD OF LAW OF MOSES

"Remember His covenant forever, The word which He commanded to a thousand generations, [16] *The covenant* which He made with Abraham, And His oath to Isaac." - 1 Chronicles 16:15-16

According to 1 Chronicles 16:15-16, even though the tabernacle and all its services and laws were established through the covenant with Moses, who's covenant does David tell Asaph and the priests to remember during their services in the tabernacle of David?

"The Scripture, foreseeing that God would justify the Gentiles by faith, preached the gospel beforehand to Abraham, *saying*, "All the nations will be blessed in you.[9] So then those who are of faith are blessed with Abraham, the believer. [10] For as many as are of the works of the Law are under a curse; for it is written, "Cursed is everyone who does not abide by all things written in the book of the law, to perform them." [11] Now that no one is justified by the Law before God is evident; for, "The righteous man shall live by faith." [12] However, the Law is not of faith; on the contrary, "He who practices them shall live by them." [13] Christ redeemed us from the curse of the Law, having become a curse for us—for it is written, "Cursed is everyone who hangs on a tree"— [14] in order that in Christ Jesus the blessing of Abraham might come to the Gentiles, so that we would receive the promise of the Spirit through faith." - Galatians 3:8-14

According to Galatians 3:8, what was preached to Abraham and what was the message?

According to Galatians 3:9-14 tell you about the covenant of Abraham verses the Covenant of Moses?

"For the promise to Abraham or to his descendants that he would be heir of the world was not through the Law, but through the righteousness of faith. [14] For if those who are of the Law are heirs, faith is made void and the promise is nullified; [15] for the Law brings about wrath, but where there is no law, there also is no violation." - Romans 4:13-15

This is really significant. The book of Galatians talks about how the Gospel itself was preached long before Christ came on the seen to Abraham! It is saying that David agreed with the Gospel to Abraham. That righteousness is through faith in the Messiah, not through the law. David got it! David saw something that few of the prophets even saw. He was a man after God's own heart! David was not as concerned with observing all the laws as much as he was concerned with the joyful service of faith. David knew that God was seeking faith filled obedience and not repetitious religious sacrifice. Could this be the continuation of the royal priesthood of *Melchizedek*?

So far we have seen that the tabernacle of David was about joyful exuberant worship and that the focus was more the faith and covenant of Abraham and not necessarily the law of Moses. These both signify a difference in position from which the priest ministered. Under the tabernacle and Law of Moses, the priests were positioned as sinners, who dwelt far from God and who entered into the presence of God from a place of violation of law, hoping to offer sacrifices in order to appease

His anger. Under the tabernacle of David, the priests are positioned as righteous, coming FROM the presence of God, intoxicated on his goodness and full of joy and thanksgiving.

3. A PLACE FOR ALL NATIONS

"Tell of His glory among the nations, His wonderful deeds among all the peoples" (1 Chronicles 16:24). In this passage we see David reveal another central theme of ministry within his Tabernacle. It is a heart for the nations.

When the temple is described as a "House of Prayer for all Nations," it is not as much saying the house of prayer is the place the holy people of God come to pray for the Nations, but the house of God is a place where all Nations are welcomed to come and pray. It is a central place of UNITING THE NATIONS. This is God's heart more so than anything!

"In that day I will raise up the fallen booth of David, And wall up its breaches; I will also raise up its ruins And rebuild it as in the days of old; ^{12} That they may possess the remnant of Edom And all the nations who are called by My name," Declares the Lord who does this." - Amos 9:11-12

In Amos 9:11-12, What is the desired result that God has for restoring the tent of David in the New Covenant?

If we remember the passage in Acts 15, James agrees by remembering Amos' prophecy, 'After these things I will return, And I will rebuild the tabernacle of David which has fallen, And I will rebuild its ruins, And I will restore it, [17] So that the rest of mankind may seek the Lord, And all the Gentiles who are called by My name' (Acts 15:16-18).

James was responding to the fact that the multitudes of Gentiles were getting baptized in the Spirit just by faith in Christ without the observance of Moses' law. Apparently the faith in the Gospel of Christ makes you clean enough for the Holy Spirit regardless of your observance of the law of Moses. That being said, we are still to honor the law of Moses, for that is what Christ did.

We see here the heart of God for His family. There are countless passages on unity that we could use to support this point. Just as the Galatians 3:8 passage says, the gospel that was preached to Abraham is that through his Seed, Jesus Christ, <u>all the families</u> of the earth would be brought into one family in God. The Tabernacle of David had an ecumenical heart. God wanted to make one people out of every people and every nation on earth. Today that would include *every denomination, every nation, and every culture.*

"Even those I will bring to My holy mountain And make them joyful in My house of prayer. Their burnt offerings and their sacrifices will be acceptable on My altar; For My house will be called a house of prayer for all the peoples." - Isaiah 56:7

What does Isaiah 56:7 tell you was Isaiah's revelation about what ministry in the house of God was supposed to look like and who would be using the house for prayer?

"And He said to them, "It is written, 'My house shall be called a house of prayer'; but you are making it a robbers' den." - Matthew 21:13

In Matthew 21:13, we see Jesus in what is possibly His most angry moment described in the Gospels. What does He say?

The House of God is a place where people from every background, nation, religion and affiliation are welcome to come worship and recognize the provision of God through His Son, Jesus Christ.

4. PERPETUAL JOY & PRAISE

Under the Law of Moses, the priests had daily ministries and sacrifices but the people in general came once a year to sacrifice and make atonement for sin. When David became King, there were only a few priests in Jerusalem. Most of the priests were scattered all over the nation. David immediately called them all to Jerusalem. By the time David died, it is estimated that there were over 4000 priests in Jerusalem, ministering in the tabernacle.

"So he left Asaph and his relatives there before the ark of the covenant of the Lord to minister before the ark continually, as every day's work required" - 1 Chronicles 16:37

Keep in mind that this was all new. In the old, the purpose of the priesthood was to make atonement for sin. They went in and went out and that was it. But now, there is perpetual joy, adoration and thanksgiving in the presence of God!

This is an entire different atmosphere and environment! It was one where it was easy to spend time. One where everyone liked coming into the presence of God. It was a happy place.

Realize that the fulfillment of the tabernacle of David was not another tabernacle of David, but instead, Gentiles being filled by the Spirit of God! God's aim was not as much to give us a model for ministry as much as it was to give us a picture of our own identity, regardless of the style of worship we employed. We are the tabernacle of David as we are filled with the joy of His Spirit perpetually!

No wonder God chose wine as the object that represents Christ's blood. We are called to be the happiest, merriest, most intoxicated people on earth - Perpetually!

NOTE: For David, the tabernacle was kind of his plan B. Is original desire was to build God a Temple, or a permanent dwelling place. God didn't allow him to because he had killed so many people so the tabernacle of David was the result. God had told David that instead of him building God a house, David's heir would be the one to build Him a house (2 Samuel 7:1-7, 11-17). David's son, Solomon ended up finishing his father's work and during his reign as king, Solomon completed the building of the temple of his father David (2 Chronicles 2-6). After the dedication of the temple it was said to be the very House of God. God was said to dwell there. It was the portal. The portal between heaven and earth and the place God came and went to and from. "In my distress I called upon the Lord, Yes, I cried to my God; And from His temple He heard my voice, And my cry for help came into His ears." - 2 Samuel 22:7 We won't go into detail here about Solomon's temple as it is very similar to Moses'.

DAVID'S CONCLUSION

So we can conclude the following things about God's dwelling place from Jacob's Vision:

* In God's house the priests (servants) obey internal faith in the order of Melchizedek and Abraham more so than they obey external laws in the order of Aaron and the Levites.
* In God's house the priests (servants) primarily offer sacrifices of Joy, Praise, and Thanksgiving.
* God's house is very inclusive, desiring to accept and honor priests (servants) from every nation and family!
* God's house is a perpetual party! His priests (servants) hardly ever sleep because they are having so much fun!

THE NEW COVENANT TABERNACLE

In the following scriptures, please highlight the words having to do with God dwelling in the corporate body of the Church:

"So then you are no longer strangers and aliens, but you are fellow citizens with the saints, and are of God's household, 20 having been built on the foundation of the apostles and prophets, Christ Jesus Himself being the corner stone, 21 in whom the whole building, being fitted together, is growing into a holy temple in the Lord, 22 in whom you also are being built together into a dwelling of God in the Spirit." - Ephesians 2:19-22

"And coming to Him as to a living stone which has been rejected by men, but is choice and precious in the sight of God, 5 you also, as living stones, are

being built up as a spiritual house for a holy priesthood, to offer up spiritual sacrifices acceptable to God through Jesus Christ." - 1 Peter 2:4-5

In the following scriptures, please highlight the words having to do with God dwelling in you as an individual:

"However, you are not in the flesh but in the Spirit, if indeed the Spirit of God dwells in you. But if anyone does not have the Spirit of Christ, he does not belong to Him. [10] If Christ is in you, though the body is dead because of sin, yet the spirit is alive because of righteousness. [11] But if the Spirit of Him who raised Jesus from the dead dwells in you, He who raised Christ Jesus from the dead will also give life to your mortal bodies through His Spirit who dwells in you." - Romans 8:9-11

"Do you not know that you are a temple of God and *that* the Spirit of God dwells in you?" - 1 Corinthians 3:16

"Or what agreement has the temple of God with idols? For we are the temple of the living God; just as God said,"I will dwell in them and walk among them; And I will be their God, and they shall be My people." - 2 Corinthians 6:16

"But Christ *was faithful* as a Son over His house— whose house we are, if we hold fast our confidence and the boast of our hope firm until the end." - Hebrews 3:6

"Or do you think that the Scripture speaks to no purpose: "He jealously desires the Spirit which He has made to dwell in us?" - James 4:5

"You are from God, little children, and have overcome them; because greater is He who is in you than he who is in the world." - 1 John 4:4

"¹² No one has seen God at any time; if we love one another, God abides in us, and His love is perfected in us. ¹³ By this we know that we abide in Him and He in us, because He has given us of His Spirit. ¹⁴ We have seen and testify that the Father has sent the Son *to be* the Savior of the world. ¹⁵ Whoever confesses that Jesus is the Son of God, God abides in him, and he in God. ¹⁶ We have come to know and have believed the love which God has for us. God is love, and the one who abides in love abides in God, and God abides in him." - 1 John 4:12-16

"Behold, I stand at the door and knock; if anyone hears My voice and opens the door, I will come in to him and will dine with him, and he with Me." - Revelation 3:20

As you can see from the passages above, we are called to be the dwelling place of God. The place where heaven meets earth. The portal through which the angels travel to and from God's presence on their mission to perform His word. You are the place people can go to in order to have an encounter with God! Christianity is not as much about what we can do for God, but what He can do through us. It is not as much about going to heaven when you die, but heaven coming to earth through you while you are alive!

When the House of God becomes more a thing you are instead of a place you go, and your place of worship becomes more a lifestyle then a building, your world will be radically transformed.

The House of God is not as much about entertaining the people of God as it is entertaining God as a person. Christianity is not about what we can do for God, but what He can do through us.

PUTTING IT ALL TOGETHER

So understanding that the ultimate destination and fulfillment of the "House of God" is Christ in His Church, we can now look back at the revelations of Jacob, Moses and David and realize they were seeing spiritual versions of us. They were getting glimpses of us through heavens eyes. In some ways their versions might seem even more accurate, complete and pure than the realities we are now experiencing as the fulfillment of those things. Looking back, we might now find ways in which their vision helps us to realize the fullness of our potential and purpose as the Bride of Christ.

Taking the revelations we learned about the house of God from Jacob, Moses and David, we can discover a lot about who we are.

FROM JACOB'S REVELATION: WHO WE ARE:

* We (the Church) are the portal through which angels travel to and from their assignments.
* We are the place through which God's voice can be heard.
* We are the place God comes and goes from.
* We are the place where He is present whether we know it or not.
* We are a place of rest in His presence

FROM MOSES' REVELATION: WHO WE ARE:

* We are a Gate or Veil = Jesus as the Door, Barrier, Doorway, threshold or Entrance to the true depths of our identity

* We are a Brazen Alter = Jesus as the Sacrifice on the Cross that removes your guilt and cleanses your conscience from all sins effects.
* We are a Bronze Laver = Jesus as the Word and True Mirror of our identity where we wash in the Sea of His Love & Power.
* We are a Table of Showbread = Communion, Inclusion in the New Covenant in the Bread of His body and the Cup of His blood.
* We are a Lampstand of "Pure Hammered Gold" = The Church with the Anointing (Christ) in us and the Spirit upon us giving light to His glory.
* We are an Altar of Incense = The Prayers and intercessions of Christ and His people.
* We are an Ark = The Throne of God, The place of His Testimony (Stone Tablets / Holy Spirit), His Provision (manna), and New Life from His Voice (Aarons Staff)

FROM DAVID'S REVELATION: WHO WE ARE:

* In God's house the priests (servants) obey internal faith in the order of Melchizedek and Abraham more so than they obey external laws in the order of Aaron and the Levites.
* In God's house the priests (servants) primarily offer sacrifices of Joy, Praise, and Thanksgiving.
* God's house is very inclusive, desiring to accept and honor priests (servants) from every nation and family!

* God's house is a perpetual party! His priests (servants) hardly ever sleep because they are having so much fun!

LANGUAGE of GOD SERIES
BOOK ONE

GOD SPEAKS

This book has five chapters that set the stage for all the other books. It focuses on opening its readers to all of the potential ways God speaks. As all the other books deal with recognizing and interpreting God's speech, book one ays the foundation and framework for good doctrine and healthy interpretation.

CHAPTER one is, "You must be Born Again" aims to remove presumptions about the ways God might communicate and introduces them to the foundational yet often unknown ways through which God has and continues to speak. **CHAPTER two** is, "God Speaks through His Scripture" and shows students how to search the scriptures both to obtain God's general thoughts (theology) as well as to obtain faith. **CHAPTER three** is, "God Speaks through His Spirit" and shows students how normal hearing directly from the Spirit should be. **CHAPTER four** is, "God Speaks through His Son," and aims to establish the foundation of all good interpretation which is Christ Himself, the ultimate source of understanding God. **CHAPTER five** is, "His Word Empowers" and shows students all the things promised to those who hear and act on God's words.

LANGUAGE of GOD SERIES

BOOK TWO

GOD SPEAKS
through
HEBREW CULTURE

Many Christians don't realize that Jesus was a Jewish Rabbi and the Bible, including the New Testament, is a Jewish work. The information in this book will unlock huge portions of the mysteries of the scriptures. With six sections aiming to expose its readers to the Hebrew context of Christ and the entire New Testament, this book is an essential foundation for sound prophetic interpretation.

CHAPTER one is, "God speaks through Rabbinic Culture" and shows reveals the historical context of many of the words and actions of Christ. **CHAPTER two** is, "God Speaks through Patriarchs and Prophets" and reveals how God used the lives of the Old Testament Patriarchs and Prophets to speak to us as prophetic pictures and parables of Christ and man. **CHAPTER three** deals with the Ancient Hebrew concept of Covenant and how covenant terminology and understanding is the heart of all ancient Hebrew and biblical culture. **CHAPTER four** is, "God Speaks through Letters, Numbers and Word pictures" and shows students how to hear God through the Hebrew Aleph-Bet and calendar. **CHAPTER five** is, "He Speaks through His feasts" and offers understanding into the prophetic nature of the seven feasts of Israel. **CHAPTER six** is, "He Speaks through His House" showing how to understand God through the places He chooses to dwell.

LANGUAGE of GOD SERIES
BOOK THREE
GOD SPEAKS
through
CREATION

"The universe was formed at God's command, so that what is seen was not made out of what was visible." (Heb.11:3) Some might assume that everything was made from nothing, as if God was nothing. We were and sometimes are still blind to Who created us and often blind to what blueprint or pattern He used. This book reveals how God embedded His mind in matter and created the natural world as a reflection of the spiritual world in order to communicate His thoughts toward us. "The works of the LORD are great, Studied by all who have pleasure in them" (Ps.111:2). This book offers a framework for hearing and seeing God through creation and offers another essential foundation for good interpretation.

CHAPTER one is, "He Speaks through Earthly Signs and Wonders" and reveals how God uses His creation as parables to speak to us. **CHAPTER two** is, "He Speaks through Symbols and Types" and offers a prophetic dictionary of biblical symbols and types that will be useful for interpreting dreams and visions. **CHAPTER three** is, "He Speaks through the Heavens" and offers students understanding into the ancient Hebrew understanding of heavenly signs, wonders and symbolism of the moon, planets and stars. **CHAPTER four** is, "He Speaks through His Stars" and deals with understanding how God has revealed the Gospel and many other things to us through His layout of the constellations.

LANGUAGE of GOD SERIES
BOOK FOUR

GOD SPEAKS
through
MEN & ANGELS

As the first three books in this series revealed the universal ways that God has spoken to all of mankind, this fourth and final book reveals the personal ways through which God speaks to each of us as individuals. He speaks through His Spirit.

CHAPTER one is, "He Speaks by His Spirit" and reveals how God lives inside of us and loves to speak directly into our thoughts and minds. **CHAPTER two** is, "He Speaks through His Gifts" and shows how God loves to use His gifts of the Spirit in and out of Church gatherings to communicate and demonstrate His word of love to us. **CHAPTER three** is, "He Speaks through Visions" and shows the biblical examples of those who heard God speak through Visions as well as a biblical framework for recognizing and interpreting your own visions. **CHAPTER four** is, "He Speaks through Dreams" and offers many biblical examples of those who had divinely inspired dreams and helps students obtain a biblical framework for interpreting their own. **CHAPTER five** is, "He Speaks through Angels" showing students the many biblical examples of God using Angles to speak and shows students how to recognize and invite Angelic activity in their own lives.

SCHOOL OF JESUS PUBLICATIONS

FOR OTHER BOOKS & RESOURCES

BY JACOB REEVE, GO TO:

www.JACOBREEVE.com

Made in the USA
Las Vegas, NV
21 February 2023

67903850R00156